Shakespeare's

The Tempest

About the Author

Matthew C. Hansen has a B.A. in English from Washington & Lee University and an M.Phil. with a concentration on Shakespeare and Early Modern Drama from University College, Oxford. He has taught literature and directed productions of Shakespeare in England and the United States including, most recently, a production of *The Tempest*. He is currently a Ph.D. candidate at the University of Nebraska at Lincoln where he holds a teaching fellowship.

Publisher's Acknowledgments
Editorial

Project Editor: Elizabeth Netedu Kuball
Acquisitions Editor: Gregory W. Tubach
Editorial Director: Kristin A. Cocks
Illustrator: DD Dowden
Special Help: Michelle Hacker

Production

Indexer: Glassman Indexing Services
Proofreader: Jeannie Smith
IDG Books Indianapolis Production Department

CliffsComplete *The Tempest*
Published by
IDG Books Worldwide, Inc.
An International Data Group Company
919 E. Hillsdale Blvd.
Suite 400
Foster City, CA 94404
www.idgbooks.com (IDG Books Worldwide Web site)
www.cliffsnotes.com (CliffsNotes Web site)

Library of Congress Control No.: 00-101105

ISBN: 0-7645-8576-2

Printed in the United States of America

10 9 8 7 6 5 4 3 2 1

1O/QU/QV/QQ/IN

Distributed in the United States by IDG Books Worldwide, Inc.

Distributed by CDG Books Canada Inc. for Canada; by Transworld Publishers Limited in the United Kingdom; by IDG Norge Books for Norway; by IDG Sweden Books for Sweden; by IDG Books Australia Publishing Corporation Pty. Ltd. for Australia and New Zealand; by TransQuest Publishers Pte Ltd. for Singapore, Malaysia, Thailand, Indonesia, and Hong Kong; by Gotop Information Inc. for Taiwan; by ICG Muse, Inc. for Japan; by Intersoft for South Africa; by Eyrolles for France; by International Thomson Publishing for Germany, Austria and Switzerland; by Distribuidora Cuspide for Argentina; by LR International for Brazil; by Galileo Libros for Chile; by Ediciones ZETA S.C.R. Ltda. for Peru; by WS Computer Publishing Corporation, Inc., for the Philippines; by Contemporanea de Ediciones for Venezuela; by Express Computer Distributors for the Caribbean and West Indies; by Micronesia Media Distributor, Inc. for Micronesia; by Chips Computadoras S.A. de C.V. for Mexico; by Editorial Norma de Panama S.A. for Panama; by American Bookshops for Finland.

For general information on IDG Books Worldwide's books in the U.S., please call our Consumer Customer Service department at 800-762-2974. For reseller information, including discounts and premium sales, please call our Reseller Customer Service department at 800-434-3422.

For information on where to purchase IDG Books Worldwide's books outside the U.S., please contact our International Sales department at 317-596-5530 or fax 317-572-4002.

For consumer information on foreign language translations, please contact our Customer Service department at 1-800-434-3422, fax 317-572-4002, or e-mail rights@idgbooks.com.

For information on licensing foreign or domestic rights, please phone +1-650-653-7098.

For sales inquiries and special prices for bulk quantities, please contact our Order Services department at 800-434-3422 or write to the address above.

For information on using IDG Books Worldwide's books in the classroom or for ordering examination copies, please contact our Educational Sales department at 800-434-2086 or fax 317-572-4005.

For press review copies, author interviews, or other publicity information, please contact our Public Relations department at 650-653-7000 or fax 650-653-7500.

For authorization to photocopy items for corporate, personal, or educational use, please contact Copyright Clearance Center, 222 Rosewood Drive, Danvers, MA 01923, or fax 978-750-4470.

 is a registered trademark under exclusive license to IDG Books Worldwide, Inc. from International Data Group, Inc.

CLIFFSCOMPLETE

Shakespeare's

The Tempest

WITHDRAWN

CONTENTS AT A GLANCE

CLIFFSCOMPLETE

Shakespeare's

The Tempest

TABLE OF CONTENTS

Shakespeare's
THE TEMPEST

INTRODUCTION TO WILLIAM SHAKESPEARE

William Shakespeare, or the "Bard" as people fondly call him, permeates almost all aspects of our society. He can be found in our classrooms, on our televisions, in our theatres, and in our cinemas. Speaking to us through his plays, Shakespeare comments on his life and culture, as well as our own. Actors still regularly perform his plays on the modern stage and screen. The 1990s, for example, saw the release of cinematic versions of *Romeo and Juliet, Hamlet, Othello, A Midsummer Night's Dream,* and many more of his works.

In addition to the popularity of Shakespeare's plays as he wrote them, other writers have modernized his works to attract new audiences. For example, *West Side Story* places *Romeo and Juliet* in New York City, and *A Thousand Acres* sets *King Lear* in Iowa corn country. Beyond adaptations and productions, his life and works have captured our cultural imagination. The twentieth century witnessed the production of a play about two minor characters from Shakespeare's *Hamlet* in *Rosencrantz and Guildenstern Are Dead* and a fictional movie about Shakespeare's early life and poetic inspiration in *Shakespeare in Love.*

Despite his monumental presence in our culture, Shakespeare remains enigmatic. He does not tell us which plays he wrote alone, on which plays he collaborated with other playwrights, or which versions of his plays to read and perform. Furthermore, with only a handful of documents available about his life,

he does not tell us much about Shakespeare the person, forcing critics and scholars to look to historical references to uncover the true-life great dramatist.

Anti-Stratfordians — modern scholars who question the authorship of Shakespeare's plays — have used this lack of information to argue that William Shakespeare either never existed or, if he did exist, did not write any of the plays we attribute to him. They believe that another historical figure, such as Francis Bacon or Queen Elizabeth I, used the name as a cover. Whether or not a man named

An engraved portrait of Shakespeare by an unknown artist, ca. 1607.
Culver Pictures, Inc./SuperStock

William Shakespeare ever actually existed is ultimately secondary to the recognition that the group of plays bound together by that name does exist and continues to educate, enlighten, and entertain us.

Family life

Though scholars are unsure of the exact date of Shakespeare's birth, records indicate that his parents — Mary and John Shakespeare — baptized him on April 26, 1564, in the small provincial town of Stratford-upon-Avon — so named because it sat on the banks of the Avon river. Because common practice was to baptize infants a few days after they were born, scholars generally recognize April 23, 1564, as Shakespeare's birthday. Coincidentally, April 23 is the day of St. George, the patron saint of England, as well as the day upon which Shakespeare would die 52 years later. William was the third of Mary and John's eight children and the first of four sons. The house in which scholars believe Shakespeare to have been born stands on Henley Street and, despite many modifications over the years, you can still visit it today.

Shakespeare's father

Prior to Shakespeare's birth, John Shakespeare lived in Snitterfield, where he married Mary Arden, the daughter of his landlord. After moving to Stratford in 1552, he worked as a glover, a moneylender, and a dealer in agricultural products such as wool and grain. He also pursued public office and achieved a variety of posts including bailiff, Stratford's highest elected position — equivalent to a small town's mayor. At the height of his career, sometime near 1576, he petitioned the Herald's Office for a coat of arms and thus the right to be a gentleman. But the rise from the middle class to the gentry did not come right away, and the costly petition expired without being granted.

Shakespeare's birthplace.
SuperStock

About this time, John Shakespeare mysteriously fell into financial difficulty. He became involved in serious litigation, was assessed heavy fines, and even lost his seat on the town council. Some scholars suggest that this decline could have resulted from religious discrimination because the Shakespeare family may have supported Catholicism, the practice of which was illegal in England. However, other scholars point out that not all religious dissenters (both Catholics and radical Puritans) lost their posts due to their religion. Whatever the cause of his decline, John did regain some prosperity toward the end of his life. In 1596, the Herald's Office granted the Shakespeare family a coat of arms at the petition of William, by now a successful playwright in London. And John, prior to his death in 1601, regained his seat on Stratford's town council.

Childhood and education

Our understanding of William Shakespeare's childhood in Stratford is primarily speculative because children do not often appear in the legal records from which many scholars attempt to reconstruct Shakespeare's life. Based on his father's local prominence, scholars speculate that Shakespeare most likely attended King's New School, a school that usually employed Oxford graduates and was generally well respected. Shakespeare would have started *petty school* — the rough equivalent to modern preschool — at the age of four or five. He would have learned to read on a *hornbook*, which was a sheet of parchment or paper on which the alphabet and the Lord's Prayer were written. This sheet was framed in wood and covered with a transparent piece of horn for durability. After two years in petty school, he would have transferred to grammar school, where his school day would have probably lasted from 6 or 7 o'clock in the morning (depending on the time of year) until 5 o'clock in the evening, with only a handful of holidays.

While in grammar school, Shakespeare would primarily have studied Latin, reciting and reading the works of classical Roman authors such as Plautus, Ovid, Seneca, and Horace. Traces of these authors' works can be seen in his dramatic texts. Toward his last years in grammar school, Shakespeare would have acquired some basic skills in Greek as well. Thus the remark made by Ben Jonson, Shakespeare's well-educated friend and contemporary playwright, that Shakespeare knew "small Latin and less Greek" is accurate. Jonson is not saying that when Shakespeare left grammar school he was only semi literate; he merely indicates that Shakespeare did not attend University, where he would have gained more Latin and Greek instruction.

Wife and children

When Shakespeare became an adult, the historical records documenting his existence began to increase. In November 1582, at the age of 18, he married 26-year-old Anne Hathaway from the nearby village of Shottery. The disparity in their ages, coupled with the fact that they baptized their first daughter, Susanna, only six months later in May 1583, has caused a great deal of modern speculation about the nature of their relationship. However, sixteenth-century conceptions of marriage differed slightly from our modern notions. Though all marriages needed to be performed before a member of the clergy,

many of Shakespeare's contemporaries believed that a couple could establish a relationship through a premarital contract by exchanging vows in front of witnesses. This contract removed the social stigma of pregnancy before marriage. (Shakespeare's plays contain instances of marriage prompted by pregnancy, and *Measure for Measure* includes this kind of premarital contract.) Two years later, in February 1585, Shakespeare baptized his twins Hamnet and Judith. Hamnet died at the age of 11 when Shakespeare was primarily living away from his family in London.

For seven years after the twins' baptism, the records remain silent on Shakespeare. At some point, he traveled to London and became involved with the theatre, but he could have been anywhere between 21 and 28 years old when he did. Though some have suggested that he may have served as an assistant to a schoolmaster at a provincial school, it seems likely that he went to London to become an actor, gradually becoming a playwright and gaining attention.

The plays: On stage and in print

The next mention of Shakespeare comes in 1592 by a University wit named Robert Greene when Shakespeare apparently was already a rising actor and playwright for the London stage. Greene, no longer a successful playwright, tried to warn other University wits about Shakespeare. He wrote:

> For there is an upstart crow, beautified with our feathers, that with his "Tiger's heart wrapped in a player's hide" supposes he is as well able to bombast out a blank verse as the best of you, and, being an absolute Johannes Factotum, is in his own conceit the only Shake-scene in a country.

This statement comes at a point in time when men without a university education, like Shakespeare, were starting to compete as dramatists with the University wits. As many critics have pointed out, Greene's statement recalls a line from *3 Henry VI*, which reads, "O tiger's heart wrapped in a woman's hide!" (I.4.137). Greene's remark does not indicate that Shakespeare was generally disliked. On the contrary, another University wit, Thomas Nashe, wrote of the great theatrical success of *Henry VI*, and Henry Chettle, Greene's publisher, later printed a flattering apology to Shakespeare. What Greene's statement does show us is that Shakespeare's reputation for poetry had reached enough of a prominence to provoke the envy of a failing competitor.

A ground plan of London after the fire of 1666, drawn by Marcus Willemsz Doornik.
Guildhall Library, London/AKG, Berlin/SuperStock

In the following year, 1593, the government closed London's theatres due to an outbreak of the bubonic plague. Publication history suggests that during this closure, Shakespeare may have written his two narrative poems, *Venus and Adonis*, published in 1593, and *The Rape of Lucrece*, published in 1594. These are the only two works that Shakespeare seems to have helped into print; each carries a dedication by Shakespeare to Henry Wriothesley, Earl of Southampton.

Stage success

When the theatres reopened in 1594, Shakespeare joined the Lord Chamberlain's Men, an acting company. Though uncertain about the history of his early dramatic works, scholars believe that by this point he had written *The Two Gentlemen of Verona, The Taming of the Shrew,* the *Henry VI* trilogy, and *Titus Andronicus*. During his early years in the theatre, he primarily wrote history plays, with his romantic comedies emerging in the 1590s. Even at this early stage in his career, Shakespeare was a success. In 1597, he was able to purchase New Place, one of the two largest houses in Stratford, and secure a coat of arms for his family.

In 1597, the lease expired on the Lord Chamberlain's playhouse, called The Theatre. Because the owner of The Theatre refused to renew the lease, the acting company was forced to perform at various playhouses until the 1599 opening of the now famous Globe Theatre, which was literally built with lumber from The Theatre. (The Globe, later destroyed by fire, has recently been reconstructed in London and can be visited today.)

Recent scholars suggest that Shakespeare's great tragedy, *Julius Caesar*, may have been the first of Shakespeare's plays performed in the original playhouse. When this open-air theatre on the Thames River opened, financial papers list Shakespeare's name as one of the principal investors. Already an actor and a playwright, Shakespeare was now becoming a "Company Man." This new status allowed him to share in the profits of the theatre rather than merely getting paid for his plays, some of which publishers were beginning to release in quarto format.

Publications

A *quarto* was a small, inexpensive book typically used for leisure books such as plays; the term itself indicates that the printer folded the paper four times. The modern day equivalent of a quarto would be a paperback. In contrast, the first collected works of Shakespeare were in folio format, which means that the printer folded each sheet only once. Scholars call the collected edition of Shakespeare's works the *First Folio*. A folio was a larger and more prestigious book than a quarto, and printers generally reserved the format for works such as the Bible.

No evidence exists that Shakespeare participated in the publication of any of his plays. Members of Shakespeare's acting company printed the First Folio seven years after Shakespeare's death. Generally, playwrights wrote their works to be performed on stage, and publishing them was a novel innovation at the time. Shakespeare probably would not have thought of them as books in the way we do. In fact, as a principal investor in the acting company (which purchased the play as well as the exclusive right to perform it), he may not have even thought of them as his own. He would probably have thought of his plays as belonging to the company.

For this reason, scholars have generally characterized most quartos printed before the Folio as "bad" by arguing that printers pirated the plays and published them illegally. How would a printer have received a pirated copy of a play? The theories range from someone stealing a copy to an actor (or actors) selling the play by relating it from memory to a printer. Many times, major differences exist between a quarto version of the play and a folio version, causing uncertainty about which is Shakespeare's true creation. *Hamlet*, for example, is almost twice as long in the Folio as in quarto versions. Recently, scholars have come to realize the value of the different versions. The *Norton Shakespeare*, for example, includes all three versions of *King Lear* — the quarto, the folio, and the *conflated* version (the combination of the quarto and folio).

Prolific productions

The first decade of the 1600s witnessed the publication of additional quartos as well as the production of most of Shakespeare's great tragedies, with *Julius Caesar* appearing in 1599 and *Hamlet* in 1600–1601. After the death of Queen Elizabeth in 1603, the Lord Chamberlain's Men became the King's Men under James I, Elizabeth's successor. Around the time of this transition in the English monarchy, the famous tragedy *Othello* (1603–1604) was most likely written and performed, followed closely by *King Lear* (1605–1606), *Antony and Cleopatra* (1606), and *Macbeth* (1606) in the next two years.

Shakespeare's name also appears as a major investor in the 1609 acquisition of an indoor theatre known as the Blackfriars. This last period of Shakespeare's career, which includes plays that considered the acting conditions both at the Blackfriars and the open-air Globe theatre, consists primarily of romances or tragicomedies such as *The Winter's Tale* and *The Tempest*. On June 29, 1613, during a performance of *All is True*, or *Henry VIII*, the thatching on top of The Globe caught fire and the playhouse burned to the ground. After this incident, the King's Men moved solely into the indoor Blackfriars Theatre.

Final days

During the last years of his career, Shakespeare collaborated on a couple of plays with contemporary dramatist John Fletcher, even possibly coming out of retirement — which scholars believe began sometime in 1613 — to work on *The Two Noble Kinsmen* (1613–1614). Three years later, Shakespeare died on April 23, 1616. Though the exact cause of death remains unknown, a vicar from Stratford in the mid-seventeenth-century wrote in his diary that Shakespeare, perhaps celebrating the marriage of his daughter, Judith, contracted a fever during a night of revelry with fellow literary figures Ben Jonson and Michael Drayton. Regardless, Shakespeare may have felt his death was imminent in March of that year, because he altered his will. Interestingly, his will mentions no book or theatrical manuscripts, perhaps indicating the lack of value that he put on printed versions of his dramatic works and their status as company property.

Seven years after Shakespeare's death, John Heminge and Henry Condell, fellow members of the King's Men, published his collected works. In their preface, they claim that they are publishing the true versions of Shakespeare's plays partially as a response to the previous quarto printings of 18 of his plays, most of these with multiple printings. This folio contains 36 plays to which scholars generally add *Pericles* and *The Two Noble Kinsmen*. This volume of Shakespeare's plays began the process of constructing Shakespeare not only as England's national poet but also as a monumental figure whose plays would continue to captivate imaginations at the end of the millennium with no signs of stopping. Ben Jonson's prophetic line about Shakespeare in the First Folio — "He was not of an age, but for all time!" — certainly holds true.

Chronology of Shakespeare's plays

1590–1591	*The Two Gentlemen of Verona*
	The Taming of the Shrew
1591	*2 Henry VI*
	3 Henry VI
1592	*1 Henry VI*
	Titus Andronicus
1592–1593	*Richard III*
	Venus and Adonis
1593–1594	*The Rape of Lucrece*
1594	*The Comedy of Errors*
1594–1595	*Love's Labour's Lost*
1595	*Richard II*
	Romeo and Juliet
	A Midsummer Night's Dream
1595–1596	*Love's Labour's Won*
	(This manuscript was lost.)

1596	*King John*
1596–1597	*The Merchant of Venice*
	1 Henry IV
1597–1598	*The Merry Wives of Windsor*
	2 Henry IV
1598	*Much Ado About Nothing*
1598–1599	*Henry V*
1599	*Julius Caesar*
1599–1600	*As You Like It*
1600–1601	*Hamlet*
1601	*Twelfth Night,* or *What You Will*
1602	*Troilus and Cressida*
1593–1603	*Sonnets*
1603	*Measure for Measure*
1603–1604	*A Lover's Complaint*
	Othello
1604–1605	*All's Well That Ends Well*
1605	*Timon of Athens*
1605–1606	*King Lear*
1606	*Macbeth*
	Antony and Cleopatra
1607	*Pericles*
1608	*Coriolanus*
1609	*The Winter's Tale*
1610	*Cymbeline*
1611	*The Tempest*
1612–1613	*Cardenio* (with John Fletcher; this manuscript was lost.)
1613	*All is True,* or *Henry VIII*
1613–1614	*The Two Noble Kinsmen* (with John Fletcher)

This chronology is derived from Stanley Wells' and Gary Taylor's *William Shakespeare: A Textual Companion,* which is listed in the "Works consulted" section below.

A note on Shakespeare's language

Readers encountering Shakespeare for the first time usually find Early Modern English difficult to understand. Yet, rather than serving as a barrier to Shakespeare, the richness of this language should form part of our appreciation of the Bard.

One of the first things readers usually notice about the language is the use of pronouns. Like the King James Version of the Bible, Shakespeare's pronouns are slightly different from our own and can cause confusion. Words like "thou" (you), "thee" and "ye" (objective cases of you), and "thy" and "thine" (your/yours) appear throughout Shakespeare's plays. You may need a little time to get used to these changes. You can find the definitions for other words that commonly cause confusion in the glossary column on the right side of each page in this edition.

Iambic pentameter

Though Shakespeare sometimes wrote in prose, he wrote most of his plays in poetry, specifically *blank verse*. Blank verse consists of lines in unrhymed *iambic pentameter*. *Iambic* refers to the stress patterns of the line. An *iamb* is an element of sound that consists of two beats — the first unstressed (da) and the second stressed (DA). A good example of an iambic line is Hamlet's famous line "To be or not to be," in which you do not stress "To," "or," and "to," but you do stress "be," "not," and "be." *Pentameter* refers to the *meter* or number of stressed syllables in a line. *Penta*meter has five stressed syllables. Thus, Juliet's line "But soft, what light through yonder window breaks?" (II.2.2) is a good example of an iambic pentameter line.

Wordplay

Shakespeare's language is also verbally rich, as he, along with many dramatists of his period, had a fondness for wordplay. This wordplay often takes the forms of double meanings, called *puns*, where a word can mean more than one thing in a given context. Shakespeare often employs these puns as a way of illustrating the distance between what is on the surface — *apparent* meanings — and what meanings lie underneath. Though recognizing these puns may be difficult at first, the notes in the far right column point many of them out to you.

If you are encountering Shakespeare's plays for the first time, the following reading tips may help ease you into the plays. Shakespeare's lines were meant to be spoken; therefore, reading them aloud or speaking them should help with comprehension. Also, though most of the lines are poetic, do not forget to read complete sentences — move from period to period as well as from line to line. Although Shakespeare's language can be difficult at first, the rewards of immersing yourself in the richness and fluidity of the lines are immeasurable.

Works consulted

For more information on Shakespeare's life and works, see the following:

Bevington, David, ed. *The Complete Works of Shakespeare*. New York: Longman, 1997.

Evans, G.Blakemore, ed. *The Riverside Shakespeare*. Boston: Houghton Mifflin Co., 1997.

Greenblatt, Stephen, ed. *The Norton Shakespeare*. New York: W.W. Norton and Co., 1997.

Kastan, David Scott, ed. *A Companion to Shakespeare*. Oxford: Blackwell, 1999.

McDonald, Russ. *The Bedford Companion to Shakespeare: An Introduction with Documents*. Boston: Bedford-St. Martin's Press, 1996.

Wells, Stanley and Gary Taylor. *William Shakespeare: A Textual Companion*. New York: W.W. Norton and Co., 1997.

INTRODUCTION TO EARLY MODERN ENGLAND

William Shakespeare (1564–1616) lived during a period in England's history that people have generally referred to as the *English Renaissance*. The term *renaissance*, meaning rebirth, was applied to this period of English history as a way of celebrating what was perceived as the rapid development of art, literature, science, and politics: in many ways, the rebirth of classical Rome.

Recently, scholars have challenged the name English Renaissance on two grounds. First, some scholars argue that the term should not be used because women did not share in the advancements of English culture during this time period; their legal status was still below that of men. Second, other scholars have challenged the basic notion that this period saw a sudden explosion of culture. A rebirth of civilization suggests that the previous period of time was not civilized. This second group of scholars sees a much more gradual transition between the Middle Ages and Shakespeare's time.

Some people use the terms *Elizabethan* and *Jacobean* when referring to periods of the sixteenth and seventeenth centuries. These terms correspond to the reigns of Elizabeth I (1558–1603) and James I (1603–1625). The problem with these terms is that they do not cover large spans of time; for example, Shakespeare's life and career spans both monarchies.

Scholars are now beginning to replace *Renaissance* with the term *Early Modern* when referring to this time period, but people still use both terms interchangeably. The term *Early Modern* recognizes that this period established many of the foundations of our modern culture. Though critics still disagree about the exact dates of the period, in general, the dates range from 1450 to 1750. Thus, Shakespeare's life clearly falls within the Early Modern period.

Shakespeare's plays live on in our culture, but we must remember that Shakespeare's culture differed greatly from our own. Though his understanding of human nature and relationships seems to apply to our modern lives, we must try to understand the world he lived in so we can better understand his plays. This introduction helps you do just that. It examines the intellectual, religious, political, and social contexts of Shakespeare's work before turning to the importance of the theatre and the printing press.

Intellectual context

In general, people in Early Modern England looked at the universe, the human body, and science very differently from the way we do. But while we do not share their same beliefs, we must not think of people during Shakespeare's time as lacking in intelligence or education. Discoveries made during the Early Modern period concerning the universe and the human body provide the basis of modern science.

Cosmology

One subject we view very differently than Early Modern thinkers is cosmology. Shakespeare's contemporaries believed in the astronomy of Ptolemy, an intellectual from Alexandria in the second century A.D. Ptolemy thought that the earth stood at the center of the universe, surrounded by nine concentric rings. The celestial bodies circled the earth in the following order: the moon, Mercury, Venus, the sun, Mars, Jupiter, Saturn, and the stars. The entire system was controlled by the *primum mobile*, or Prime Mover, which initiated and maintained the movement of the celestial bodies. No one had yet discovered the last three planets in our solar system, Uranus, Neptune, and Pluto.

In 1543, Nicolaus Copernicus published his theory of a sun-based solar system, in which the sun stood at the center and the planets revolved around it. Though this theory appeared prior to Shakespeare's birth, people didn't really start to change their minds until 1610, when Galileo used his telescope to confirm Copernicus' theory. David Bevington asserts in the general introduction to his edition of Shakespeare's works that during most of Shakespeare's writing career, the cosmology of the universe was in question, and this sense of uncertainty influences some of his plays.

Universal hierarchy

Closely related to Ptolemy's hierarchical view of the universe is a hierarchical conception of the Earth (sometimes referred to as the *Chain of Being*). During the Early Modern period, many people believed that all of creation was organized hierarchically. God existed at the top, followed by the angels, men, women, animals, plants, and rocks. (Because all women were thought to exist below all men on the chain, we can easily imagine the confusion that Elizabeth I caused when she became queen of England. She was literally "out of order," an expression that still exists in our society.) Though the concept of this hierarchy is a useful one when beginning to study Shakespeare, keep in mind that distinctions in this hierarchical view were not always clear and that we should not reduce all Early Modern thinking to a simple chain.

Elements and humors

The belief in a hierarchical scheme of existence created a comforting sense of order and balance that carried over into science as well. Shakespeare's contemporaries generally accepted that four different elements composed everything in the universe: earth, air, water, and fire. People associated these four elements with four qualities of being. These qualities — hot, cold, moist, and dry — appeared in different combinations in the elements. For example, air was hot and moist; water was cold and moist; earth was cold and dry; and fire was hot and dry.

In addition, people believed that the human body contained all four elements in the form of *humors* — blood, phlegm, yellow bile, and black bile — each of which corresponded to an element. Blood corresponded to air (hot and moist), phlegm to water (cold and moist), yellow bile to fire (hot and dry), and black bile to earth (cold and dry). When someone was sick, physicians generally believed that the patient's humors were not in the proper balance. For example, if someone were diagnosed with an abundance of blood, the physician would bleed the patient (using leeches or cutting the skin) in order to restore the balance.

Shakespeare's contemporaries also believed that the humors determined personality and temperament. If a person's dominant humor was blood, he was considered light-hearted. If dominated by yellow bile (or *choler*), that person was irritable. The dominance of phlegm led a person to be dull and kind. And if black bile prevailed, he was melancholy or sad. Thus, people of Early Modern England often used the humors to explain behavior and emotional outbursts. Throughout Shakespeare's plays, he uses the concept of the humors to define and explain various characters.

A complex representation of the balance of elements can be seen in *The Tempest* in Prospero's two servants, Ariel and Caliban. Ariel is an airy spirit who can shift in shape. At times, Ariel takes the form of fire; at other times, of water or a water spirit ("nymph o' the sea"). And of course, "air" is an essential part of Ariel's name. Ariel is balanced by Caliban, who is not only earthy but labeled, insultingly, by Prospero as "earth."

Religious context

Shakespeare lived in an England full of religious uncertainty and dispute. From the Protestant Reformation to the translation of the Bible into English, the Early Modern era is punctuated with events that have greatly influenced modern religious beliefs.

The Reformation

Until the Protestant Reformation, the only Christian church was the Catholic, or "universal," church. Beginning in Europe in the early sixteenth century, religious thinkers such as Martin Luther and John Calvin, who claimed that the Roman Catholic Church had become corrupt and was no longer following the word of God, began what has become known as the *Protestant Reformation.* The Protestants ("protestors") believed in salvation by faith rather than works. They also believed in the primacy of the

Bible and advocated giving all people access to reading the Bible.

Many English people initially resisted Protestant ideas. However, the Reformation in England began in 1527 during the reign of Henry VIII, prior to Shakespeare's birth. In that year, Henry VIII decided to divorce his wife, Catherine of Aragon, for her failure to produce a male heir. (Only one of their children, Mary, survived past infancy.) Rome denied Henry's petitions for a divorce, forcing him to divorce Catherine without the Church's approval, which he did in 1533.

A portrait of King Henry VIII, artist unknown, ca. 1542.
National Portrait Gallery, London/SuperStock

The Act of Supremacy

The following year, the Pope excommunicated Henry VIII while Parliament confirmed his divorce and the legitimacy of his new marriage through the *Act of Succession*. Later in 1534, Parliament passed the *Act of Supremacy*, naming Henry the "Supreme Head of the Church in England." Henry continued to persecute both radical Protestant reformers and Catholics who remained loyal to Rome.

Henry VIII's death in 1547 brought Edward VI, his 10-year-old son by Jane Seymour (the king's third wife), to the throne. This succession gave Protestant reformers the chance to solidify their break with the Catholic Church. During Edward's reign, Archbishop Thomas Cranmer established the foundation for the Anglican Church through his 42 articles of religion. He also wrote the first *Book of Common Prayer*, adopted in 1549, which was the official text for worship services in England.

Bloody Mary

Catholics continued to be persecuted until 1553, when the sickly Edward VI died and was succeeded by Mary, his half-sister and the Catholic daughter of Catherine of Aragon. The reign of Mary witnessed the reversal of religion in England through the restoration of Catholic authority and obedience to Rome. Protestants were executed in large numbers, which earned the monarch the nickname *Bloody Mary*. Many Protestants fled to Europe to escape persecution.

Elizabeth, the daughter of Henry VIII and Anne Boleyn, outwardly complied with the mandated Catholicism during her half-sister Mary's reign, but she restored Protestantism when she took the throne in 1558 after Mary's death. Thus, in the space of single decade, England's throne passed from Protestant to Catholic to Protestant, with each change carrying serious and deadly consequences.

Though Elizabeth reigned in relative peace from 1558 to her death in 1603, religion was still a serious concern for her subjects. During Shakespeare's life, a great deal of religious dissent existed in England. Many Catholics, who remained loyal to Rome and their church, were persecuted for their beliefs. At the other end of the spectrum, the Puritans were persecuted for their belief that the Reformation was not complete. (The English pejoratively applied the term *Puritan* to religious groups that wanted to continue purifying the English church by such measures as removing the *episcopacy*, or the structure of bishops.)

The Great Bible

One thing agreed upon by both the Anglicans and Puritans was the importance of a Bible written in English. Translated by William Tyndale in 1525, the first authorized Bible in English, published in 1539, was known as the Great Bible. This Bible was later revised during Elizabeth's reign into what was known as the Bishop's Bible. As Stephen Greenblatt points out in his introduction to the *Norton Shakespeare*, Shakespeare would probably have been familiar with both the Bishop's Bible, heard aloud in Mass, and the Geneva Bible, which was written by English exiles in Geneva. The last authorized Bible produced during Shakespeare's lifetime came within the last decade of his life when James I's commissioned edition, known as the King James Bible, appeared in 1611.

Political context

Politics and religion were closely related in Shakespeare's England. Both of the monarchs under whom Shakespeare lived had to deal with religious and political dissenters.

Elizabeth I

Despite being a Protestant, Elizabeth I tried to take a middle road on the religious question. She allowed Catholics to practice their religion in private as long as they outwardly appeared Anglican and remained loyal to the throne.

Elizabeth's monarchy was one of absolute supremacy. Believing in the divine right of kings, she styled herself as being appointed by God to rule England. To oppose the Queen's will was the equivalent of opposing God's will. Known as *passive obedience*, this doctrine did not allow any opposition even to a tyrannical monarch because God had appointed the king or queen for reasons unknown to His subjects on earth. However, as Bevington notes, Elizabeth's power was not as absolute as her rhetoric suggested. Parliament, already well established in England, reserved some power, such as the authority to levy taxes, for itself.

A portrait of Elizabeth I by George Gower, ca. 1588.
National Portrait Gallery, London/SuperStock

Elizabeth I lived in a society that restricted women from possessing any political or personal autonomy and power. As queen, Elizabeth violated and called into question many of the prejudices and practices against women. In a way, her society forced her to "overcome" her sex in order to rule effectively. However, her position did nothing to increase the status of women in England.

One of the rhetorical strategies that Elizabeth adopted in order to rule effectively was to separate her position as monarch of England from her natural body — to separate her *body politic* from her *body natural*. In addition, throughout her reign, Elizabeth brilliantly negotiated between domestic and foreign factions — some of whom were anxious about a female monarch and wanted her to marry — appeasing both sides without ever committing to one.

She remained unmarried throughout her 45-year reign, partially by styling herself as the Virgin Queen whose purity represented England herself. Her refusal to marry and her habit of hinting and promising marriage with suitors both foreign and domestic helped Elizabeth maintain internal and external peace. Not marrying allowed her to retain her independence, but it left the succession of the English throne in question. In 1603, on her deathbed, she named James VI, King of Scotland and son of her cousin Mary, as her successor.

James I

When he assumed the English crown, James VI of Scotland became James I of England. (Some historians refer to him as James VI and I.) Like Elizabeth, James was a strong believer in the divine right of kings and their absolute authority.

Upon his arrival in London to claim the English throne, James made his plans to unite Scotland and England clear. However, a long-standing history of enmity existed between the two countries. Partially as a result of this history and the influx of Scottish courtiers into English society, anti-Scottish prejudice abounded in England. When James asked Parliament for the title of "King of Great Britain," he was denied.

As scholars such as Bevington have pointed out, James was less successful than Elizabeth was in negotiating between the different religious and political factions in England. Although he was a Protestant,

he began to have problems with the Puritan sect of the House of Commons, which ultimately led to a rift between the court (which also started to have Catholic sympathies) and the Parliament. This rift between the monarchy and Parliament eventually escalated into the civil war that would erupt during the reign of James' son, Charles I.

In spite of its difficulties with Parliament, James' court was a site of wealth, luxury, and extravagance. James I commissioned elaborate feasts, masques, and pageants, and in doing so he more than doubled the royal debt. Stephen Greenblatt suggests that Shakespeare's *The Tempest* may reflect this extravagance through Prospero's magnificent banquet and accompanying masque. Reigning from 1603 to 1625, James I remained the King of England throughout the last years of Shakespeare's life.

Social context

Shakespeare's England divided itself roughly into two social classes: the aristocrats (or nobility) and everyone else. The primary distinctions between these two classes were ancestry, wealth, and power. Simply put, the aristocrats were the only ones who possessed all three.

Aristocrats were born with their wealth, but the growth of trade and the development of skilled professions began to provide wealth for those not born with it. Although the notion of a middle class did not begin to develop until after Shakespeare's death, the possibility of some social mobility did exist in Early Modern England. Shakespeare himself used the wealth gained from the theatre to move into the lower ranks of the aristocracy by securing a coat of arms for his family.

Shakespeare was not unique in this movement, but not all people received the opportunity to increase their social status. Members of the aristocracy feared this social movement and, as a result, promoted harsh laws of apprenticeship and fashion, restricting certain styles of dress and material. These laws dictated that only the aristocracy could wear certain articles of clothing, colors, and materials. Though enforcement was a difficult task, the Early Modern aristocracy considered dressing above one's station a moral and ethical violation.

The status of women

The legal status of women did not allow them much public or private autonomy. English society functioned on a system of patriarchy and hierarchy (see "Universal hierarchy" earlier in this introduction), which means that men controlled society beginning with the individual family. In fact, the family metaphorically corresponded to the state. For example, the husband was the king of his family. His authority to control his family was absolute and based on divine right, similar to that of the country's king. People also saw the family itself differently than today, considering apprentices and servants part of the whole family.

The practice of *primogeniture* — a system of inheritance that passed all of a family's wealth through the first male child — accompanied this system of patriarchy Thus women did not generally inherit their family's wealth and titles. In the absence of a male heir, some women, such as Queen Elizabeth, did. But after women married, they lost almost all of their already limited legal rights, such as the right to inherit, to own property, and to sign contracts. In all likelihood, Elizabeth I would have lost much of her power and authority had she married.

Furthermore, women did not generally receive an education and could not enter certain professions, including acting. Instead, society relegated women to the domestic sphere of the home.

The Tempest presents a conscious contradiction to this general pattern. Miranda, although she has grown up on an isolated island, is well-educated, outspoken, and confident. She nonetheless proves a pawn in her more powerful father's political plans. Miranda's promised marriage to Ferdinand in the play, in addition to its romantic dimension, is a dynastic marriage that will bring political stability to the future generations of both Prospero and Alonso's children.

Daily life

Daily life in Early Modern England began before sunup — exactly how early depended on one's station in life. A servant's responsibilities usually included preparing the house for the day. Families usually possessed limited living space, and even among wealthy families, multiple family members tended to share a small number of rooms, suggesting that privacy may not have been important or practical.

Working through the morning, Elizabethans usually had lunch about noon. This midday meal was the primary meal of the day, much like dinner is for modern families. The workday usually ended around sundown or 5 p.m., depending on the season. Before an early bedtime, Elizabethans usually ate a light repast and then settled in for a couple of hours of reading (if the family members were literate and could bear the high cost of books) or socializing.

Mortality rates

Mortality rates in Early Modern England were high compared to our standards, especially among infants. Infection and disease ran rampant because physicians did not realize the need for antiseptics and sterile equipment. As a result, communicable diseases often spread very rapidly in cities, particularly London.

In addition, the bubonic plague frequently ravaged England, with two major outbreaks — from 1592–1594 and in 1603 — occurring during Shakespeare's lifetime. People did not understand the plague and generally perceived it as God's punishment. (We now know that the plague was spread by fleas and could not be spread directly from human to human.) Without a cure or an understanding of what transmitted the disease, physicians could do nothing to stop the thousands of deaths that resulted from each outbreak. These outbreaks had a direct effect on Shakespeare's career, because the government often closed the theatres in an effort to impede the spread of the disease.

London life

In the sixteenth century, London, though small compared to modern cities, was the largest city of Europe, with a population of about 200,000 inhabitants in the city and surrounding suburbs. London was a crowded city without a sewer system, which facilitated epidemics such as the plague. In addition, crime rates were high in the city due to inefficient law enforcement and the lack of street lighting.

Despite these drawbacks, London was the cultural, political, and social heart of England. As the home of the monarch and most of England's trade, London was a bustling metropolis. Not surprisingly, a young Shakespeare moved to London to begin his professional career.

The theatre

Most theatres were not actually located within the city of London. Rather, theatre owners built them on the south bank of the Thames River (in Southwark) across from the city in order to avoid the strict regulations that applied within the city's walls. These restrictions stemmed from a mistrust of public performances as locations of plague and riotous behavior. Furthermore, because theatre performances took place during the day, they took laborers away from their jobs. Opposition to the theatres also came from Puritans who believed that they fostered immorality.

Therefore, theatres moved out of the city, to areas near other sites of restricted activities, such as dog fighting, bear- and bull-baiting, and prostitution.

Despite the move, the theatre was not free from censorship or regulation. In fact, a branch of the government known as the Office of the Revels attempted to ensure that plays did not present politically or socially sensitive material. Prior to each performance, the Master of the Revels would read a complete text of each play, cutting out offending sections or, in some cases, not approving the play for public performance.

Performance spaces

Theatres in Early Modern England were quite different from our modern facilities. They were usually open-air, relying heavily on natural light and good weather. The rectangular stage extended out into an area that people called the *pit* — a circular, uncovered area about 70 feet in diameter. Audience members had two choices when purchasing admission to a theatre. Admission to the pit, where the lower classes (or *groundlings*) stood for the performances, was the cheaper option. People of wealth could purchase a seat in one of the three covered tiers of seats that ringed the pit. At full capacity, a public theatre in Early Modern England could hold between 2,000 and 3,000 people.

The recently reconstructed Globe Theatre.
Chris Parker/PAL

The stage, which projected into the pit and was raised about 5 feet above it, had a covered portion called the *heavens*. The heavens enclosed theatrical equipment for lowering and raising actors to and from the stage. A trapdoor in the middle of stage provided theatrical graves for characters such as Ophelia and also allowed ghosts, such as Banquo in *Macbeth*, to rise from the earth. A wall separated the back of the stage from the actors' dressing room, known as the *tiring house*. At each end of the wall stood a door for major entrances and exits. Above the wall and doors stood a gallery directly above the stage, reserved for the wealthiest spectators. Actors occasionally used this area when a performance called for a difference in height — for example, to represent Juliet's balcony or the walls of a besieged city. A good example of this type of theatre was the original Globe Theatre in London in which Shakespeare's company, The Lord Chamberlain's Men (later, the King's Men), staged its plays. However, indoor theatres, such as the Blackfriars, differed slightly because the pit was filled with chairs that faced a rectangular stage. Because only the wealthy could afford the cost of admission, the public generally considered these theatres private.

Shakespeare in Love *shows how the interior of the Globe would have appeared.*
Everett Collection

The presentation of *The Tempest* on the Jacobean stage is in many ways an exception to the pattern of rules outlined here. *The Tempest* appears to have been designed and consciously written for indoor performance and was likely performed at the Blackfriars Theatre. The play incorporates a significant amount of spectacle and, as suggested by the presence of detailed stage directions (a rarity among the original printed versions of Shakespeare's plays), it is obvious that some complex scenery and theatre machinery were probably employed in its presentation.

Actors and staging

Performances in Shakespeare's England, in general, do not appear to have employed scenery. However, theatre companies developed their costumes with great care and expense. In fact, a playing company's costumes were its most valuable items. These extravagant costumes were the object of much controversy because some aristocrats feared that the actors could use them to disguise their social status on the streets of London.

Costumes also disguised a player's gender. All actors on the stage during Shakespeare's lifetime were men. Young boys whose voices had not reached maturity played female parts. This practice no doubt influenced Shakespeare's and his contemporary playwrights' thematic explorations of cross-dressing.

Though historians have managed to reconstruct the appearance of the early modern theatre, such as the recent construction of the Globe in London, much of the information regarding how plays were performed during this era has been lost. Scholars of Early Modern theatre have turned to the scant external and internal stage directions in manuscripts in an effort to find these answers. Although a hindrance for modern critics and scholars, the lack of detail about Early Modern performances has allowed modern directors and actors a great deal of flexibility and room to be creative.

The printing press

If not for the printing press, many Early Modern plays may not have survived until today. In Shakespeare's time, printers produced all books by *sheet* — a single, large piece of paper that the printer would fold in order to produce the desired book size. For example, a folio required folding the sheet once, a quarto four times, an octavo eight, and so on. Sheets would be printed one side at a time; thus, printers had to simultaneously print multiple nonconsecutive pages.

In order to estimate what section of the text would be on each page, the printer would *cast off* copy. After the printer made these estimates, *compositors* would set the type upside down, letter by letter. This process of setting type produced textual errors, some of which a proofreader would catch. When a proofreader found an error, the compositors would fix the piece or pieces of type. Printers called corrections made after printing began *stop-press* corrections, because they literally had to stop the press to fix the error. Because of the high cost of paper, printers would still sell the sheets printed before they made the correction.

Printers placed frames of text in the bed of the printing press and used them to imprint the paper. They then folded and grouped the sheets of paper into gatherings, after which the pages were ready for sale. The buyer had the option of getting the new play bound.

The printing process was crucial to the preservation of Shakespeare's works, but the printing of drama in Early Modern England was not a standardized practice. Many of the first editions of Shakespeare's plays appear in quarto format and, until recently, scholars regarded them as "corrupt." In fact, scholars still debate how close a relationship exists between what appeared on the stage in the sixteenth and seventeenth centuries and what appears on the printed page. The inconsistent and scant appearance of stage directions, for example, makes it difficult to determine how close this relationship was.

We know that the practice of the theatre allowed the alteration of plays by a variety of hands other than the author's, further complicating any efforts to extract what a playwright wrote and what was changed by either the players, the printers, or the government censors. Theatre was a collaborative environment. Rather than lament our inability to determine authorship and what exactly Shakespeare wrote, we should work to understand this collaborative nature and learn from it.

The Tempest appears as the first play in the 1623 collection of Shakespeare's plays, the First Folio. It is an especially well-printed text and contains detailed stage directions, complete act and scene divisions, and a minimum number of errors of composition (type-setting) and punctuation.

Shakespeare wrote his plays for the stage, and the existing published texts reflect the collaborative nature of the theatre as well as the unavoidable changes made during the printing process. A play's first written version would have been the author's *foul papers*, which invariably consisted of blotted lines and revised text. From there, a scribe would recopy the play and produce a *fair copy*. The theatre manager would then copy out and annotate this copy into a playbook (what people today call a *promptbook*).

At this point, scrolls of individual parts were copied out for actors to memorize. (Due to the high cost of paper, theatre companies could not afford to provide their actors with a complete copy of the play.) The government required the company to send the playbook to the Master of the Revels, the government official who would make any necessary changes or mark any passages considered unacceptable for performance.

Printers could have used any one of these copies to print a play. We cannot determine whether a printer used the author's version, the modified theatrical version, the censored version, or a combination when printing a given play. Refer back to the "Publications" section of the Introduction to William Shakespeare for further discussion of the impact printing practices has on our understanding of Shakespeare's works.

Works cited

For more information regarding Early Modern England, consult the following works:

Bevington, David. "General Introduction." *The Complete Works of William Shakespeare.* Updated Fourth edition. New York: Longman, 1997.

Greenblatt, Stephen. "Shakespeare's World." *Norton Shakespeare.* New York: W.W. Norton and Co., 1997.

Kastan, David Scott, ed. *A Companion to Shakespeare.* Oxford: Blackwell, 1999.

McDonald, Russ. *The Bedford Companion to Shakespeare: An Introduction with Documents.* Boston: Bedford-St. Martin's Press, 1996.

INTRODUCTION TO *THE TEMPEST*

Although not, as it was once thought to be, the last play written by Shakespeare, *The Tempest* is arguably his comic masterpiece. Shakespeare's understanding of the term *comic* and of comedy itself is not what we would consider the side-splitting, laugh-a-minute type of comedy we see in films and on television today. Rather, for Shakespeare and his contemporaries, comedy followed the definition set forth by Aristotle, in which enemies are reconciled as friends and no one is killed. In romantic comedy, the form Shakespeare became renowned for with plays such as *As You Like It, Much Ado About Nothing,* and the appropriately titled *All's Well That Ends Well* (the title of which is the definition of comedy), the plays ended more often than not with a marriage.

The Tempest is far from a straightforward comedy or even a straightforward Shakespearean comedy. Coming as it does near the end of Shakespeare's career as a London playwright, the play reflects not only Shakespeare's growth and maturity as a writer but also reflects current trends in popular taste for drama and entertainment. These popular tastes include an interest in what was considered, in the early seventeenth century, a new form of drama: *tragicomedy.*

Pastoral tragicomedies were a form of popular entertainment introduced into England as adaptations and translations of Italian works in the early seventeenth century. John Fletcher, the playwright who would later collaborate with Shakespeare on at least two plays written after *The Tempest* and then go on to succeed Shakespeare as the principal playwright of the King's Men, was one of the early forces in popularizing this form of drama for the English stage. Fletcher translated and adapted both the plays and theories of the contemporary Italian playwright Giambattista Guarini concerning tragicomedy, a form of drama not sanctioned by strict purists of Classical traditions because it was not discussed by Aristotle or written by any of the great Greek or Roman writers. Fletcher's definition of tragicomedy is instructive in understanding *The Tempest* and its relationship to this emergent form of entertainment. Referring to his own play, *The Faithful Shepherdesse* (an adaptation of Guarini's *Il*

Pastor Fido or *The Faithful Shepherd*) Fletcher writes, "[B]ecause it wants death it is no tragedy, but because it brings some close to it, it is no comedy." The same could easily be said of all of Shakespeare's so-called late plays or romances — *Pericles*, *Cymbeline*, *The Winter's Tale*, and *The Tempest* — for all of these plays contain either reported deaths or near deaths (*The Winter's Tale* has two actual deaths and *Cymbeline* has a beheading), and yet all end happily, with marriage, and importantly, with a profound sense of forgiveness.

In every case, the fact that these plays end happily has something to do with magic or the influence of miraculous events. *The Tempest* in particular is a play that for four acts appears as though it may well prove to be a revenge tragedy and not a romantic comedy at all, with Prospero seeking retribution against his own brother and the other politicians who assisted in overthrowing him. The tension that Shakespeare builds up and then releases in the movement from potential tragedy to actual comedy is a perfect example of the power inherent in the tragicomic form.

The two-part structure that enables this movement also owes something to the Court Masques. Court Masques were lavish forms of entertainment that grew in both popularity and extravagance when James I acceded to the throne of England in 1603. The art form depended on lavish spectacle — ornate scenery, expensive costumes, music, and dancing. The principal roles in the masque proper were performed by the noblemen and noblewomen at court, including King James and Queen Anne, as well as the royal princes Henry and Charles and the princess Elizabeth. The masque proper symbolized the order of the universe under the good rule of the King (who was often presented as a god from classical mythology). In order to showcase the power of this order, the masque was preceded or framed by an anti-masque, a wild show consisting of disorder, discordant sound, and wild, nearly uncontrolled antics. The parts in the anti-masque were performed by professional actors.

Many of Shakespeare's contemporaries wrote masques for the King and court, but Shakespeare himself never did. All four of Shakespeare's late plays show the influence of this popular form of entertainment, however. This is most especially true in *The Tempest*, where the tragicomic form, wedded with the use of masque and anti-masque elements, results in a play that is very different from the earlier romantic comedies on which Shakespeare and his company built their reputation.

Associated with the final stages of Shakespeare's career, *The Tempest* was probably written sometime between 1610 and 1611. This date is a fairly precise one, and the evidence that provides the earliest and latest possible dates of composition is exceptionally solid. The earliest date after which Shakespeare probably began writing *The Tempest* has to do with some of the sources Shakespeare drew on; those sources, the so-called Bermuda pamphlets, are discussed in more detail in the following section. One of those pamphlets in particular, William Strachey's *True Reportory of the wracke, and redemption of Thomas Gates, Knight; upon and from the Ilands of the Bermudas; his coming to Virginia, and the estate of that Colonie then and after*, is a detailed description of the wreck of a ship called the *Sea-Adventure*, which was caught in a sea storm near the coast of the Bermuda Islands en route from England to Virginia. The letter is a report to the shareholders in the Virginia Company, the private financiers of English colonies in the New World, among whom was the Earl of Southampton, one of Shakespeare's patrons. Strachey's letter is dated July 1610, and probably arrived in England — along with other reports on the colony — in September of that year. It was not published, however, until 1625. Because of significant verbal parallels between the letter and Shakespeare's description of Prospero's island, scholars have long believed that Shakespeare read a manuscript copy of this letter sometime in either the fall or winter of 1610.

Shakespeare certainly finished *The Tempest* before Hallowmas (November 1) in 1611, when it was performed at Whitehall before King James. It was revived at Court the following winter (1612–1613), where it was performed for James' daughter, Princess Elizabeth and her husband-to-be Frederick, The Elector Palatine. (Frederick, The Elector Palatine, was the ruler of the small Palatinate of the Rhine, a Protestant stronghold surrounded by the Holy Roman Empire in what is today northern Germany. An alliance between England and this Protestant ally held tremendous political and religious cachet and was thus greatly desired by James; furthermore it has striking similarities to the benefits Prospero looks to in a marriage between Miranda and Ferdinand.) Specifics on the staging of the plays follows a brief discussion of the sources in this introduction.

The text of *The Tempest* in this volume comes from the First Folio, the first collected publication of Shakespeare's works, published in 1623. In this collection of 36 plays, *The Tempest* appears first (despite the fact that it was one of the last plays Shakespeare wrote, and probably the last play he wrote without a collaborator). Pride of place, it seems, was afforded this play and certainly the text itself bears this out. The Folio text of *The Tempest* is exemplary, with accurate punctuation, detailed stage directions, complete act and scene divisions, and a minimum of printing errors — elements of modern editorial practice that are notably lacking in other plays in the volume.

Sources for Shakespeare's play

The Tempest is unique among Shakespeare's plays in that it has no obvious source for its core story or plot line. Shakespeare was a great reviser of stories, improving on them greatly in his own version, but he was rarely an inventor of completely original work. *The Tempest*, a play in which the power of the imagination is of central importance, is a striking exception.

Shakespeare did, however, construct *The Tempest* around a number of known sources. The wreck of the *Sea-Adventure*, referred to in the *True Reportory* of William Strachey, is one contemporary incident that clearly had an effect on Shakespeare's telling of this story. It would be easy to overemphasize the importance of this and other travel reports from the time period in which Shakespeare wrote *The Tempest*, however. The dramatic use of a shipwreck was not a new idea for Shakespeare. *The Comedy of Errors*, one of Shakespeare's earliest plays, contains a shipwreck that separates twin brothers and their mother and father in its background story; *Twelfth Night* reworks this same device by providing a background story that separates twin brother and sister. Given this fact, experienced readers of Shakespeare will notice that Shakespeare uses his own earlier plays as part of his source material, especially for certain descriptions. Far from a sign of weakness, this is suggestive of how connected Shakespeare's canon truly is and how, as he developed as a playwright, he returned to his own earlier expressions of words and ideas and worked to further refine and improve upon them.

Shakespeare also turned to other texts for inspiration and likewise improved them for dramatic utterance, as the detailed commentary in this volume demonstrates. Two of these significant incidents are Shakespeare's reading of the French essayist Michel de Montaigne and his reworking of a speech spoken by Medea in Ovid's *Metamorphoses*.

Michel de Montaigne (1533–1592) traveled to Brazil in 1557 and observed the New World natives there. His comments on them in his *Essays* of 1580 (translated into English by John Florio in 1603) are clearly drawn upon by Shakespeare in Act II, Scene 1, in which Gonzalo describes his ideal commonwealth. Moreover, Montaigne writes about the distinctions between the natural world and civilization, and it is in this larger theme that the essays truly come into play as a source for Shakespeare. Ultimately, Montaigne saw the natives of the New World as noble savages; although they were unfamiliar with the laws and customs of Europe (the Old World), they nonetheless had a natural knowledge of certain fundamental principles of humanity. This caused some uproar in the Europe of Montaigne's day when it is considered that Montaigne in essence came to defend the natives' practice (or supposed practice) of cannibalism, or at the very least to question just how *civil* civilization actually is:

> I am not sorry we note the barbarous horror of such an action [i.e., cannibalism], but grieved, that prying so narrowly into their faults we are so blinded in ours. I think there is more barbarism in eating men alive, than to feed upon them being dead; to mangle by tortures and torments a body full of lively sense, to roast him in pieces, to make dogs and swine to gnaw and tear him in mammocks (as we have not only read, but seen very lately, yea in our own memory, not amongst ancient enemies, but our neighbors and fellow-citizens; and which is worse, under pretense of piety and religion) than to roast and eat him after he is dead.

Shakespeare questions society and the supposedly sophisticated and civilized in similar ways. Note the "roasting" and cruel mocks of Gonzalo that Antonio and Sebastian provide in Act II, Scene 1, and Act III, Scene 1.

In this regard, we should look also at Ovid's *Metamorphoses* (a text Shakespeare would have studied in Latin, although he clearly also knew it in the famous 1567 translation by Arthur Golding). Although Medea's speech from Book VII, in which she addresses her magical agents as "ye elves of hills, brooks, of woods alone . . ." is remarkably similar to words spoken by Prospero in Act V, Scene 1, the larger theme at work in Ovid should be considered as well. As Ovid's title, *Metamorphoses*, suggests, he

is concerned with the transformations of a person's outward shape as an indicator of their inward self or soul. As Ovid writes in Book XV:

> not all That bear the name of men . . .
> . . . Are for to be accounted men: but such as under
> awe Of reasons rule continually do live in virtue's law;
> And that the rest do differ naught from beasts, but
> rather be Much worse than beasts, because they do
> abase their own degree.

Shakespeare reworks and draws on sources in more ways than as simple verbal inspirations. He draws on core themes and reworks them in his own plays as part of the larger network of meaning and significance that his plays aim to create.

The Tempest is also indebted to Shakespeare's knowledge of Virgil's *Aeneid*, certain books of which he would have read in Latin as a schoolboy. In particular, the banquet scene (Act III, Scene 2), in which a tempting banquet appears and then disappears while Ariel appears in the form of a harpy, comes directly from a scene in Book III of Virgil's epic. As with his use of Montaigne and Ovid, however, the relationship between finished play and source material is not a simple one-to-one correspondence. Shakespeare also alludes to his knowledge of the *Aeneid* in the witty exchange in Act II, Scene 1, concerning "widow Dido" and Gonzalo's "mistake" in conflating Tunis and Carthage. Virgil deals throughout the *Aeneid* with issues of personal and corporate ambition, with loyalty to the self versus loyalty to the state or larger good. Shakespeare too takes up this issue by showing characters — notably, Prospero and his brother Antonio — who are in conflict over issues of personal ambition and desire, loyalty to tradition and expectations. Prospero has, by his own admission, made a mistake similar to that of Shakespeare's earlier creation, King Lear, in attempting to pass the details of government on to someone else (in Prospero's case, to his brother Antonio) while maintaining for himself the name and all the trappings of power that come with being Duke of Milan. This is evidence of selfishness and not what is desired or needed in a good governor. Prospero learns this, but only by being betrayed by his brother's own ambition to not only serve as the governor of Milan in practice, but in name and recognition as well.

Peter Fonda in a television version of The Tempest
Everett Collection

Performance history of *The Tempest*

There are two recorded performances of *The Tempest*, both of them Court or Royal performances. According to the Revels account for 1611, "Hallowmass night was presented at Whitehall before the King's Majesty, a play called *The Tempest*." A subsequent record of payment made to John Heminges, one of Shakespeare's partners in the King's Men, reads:

> *Item paid to John Heminges upon the Council's warrant . . . for presenting before the Princess Highness the Lady Elizabeth and the Prince Palatine Elector, fourteen several plays, viz: one play called Philaster, one called The Knot of Fools, one other Much Ado About Nothing, The Maid's Tragedy, The Merry Devil of Edmonton, The Tempest. . . .*

This second performance was, therefore, certainly part of either the betrothal (engagement) or marriage celebration for Princess Elizabeth and Frederick, The Elector Palatine. Given this second performance, the dynastic marriage Prospero orchestrates for Miranda and Ferdinand and the masque in Act IV that celebrates it take on enhanced significance.

The playing space at Whitehall, where the first and probably also the second performance noted above took place was in many ways similar to the modern theatres we are accustomed to today. Certainly this indoor theatre with scenery would be more like our modern theatres than the Globe. Special circumstances for this type of performance should also be briefly considered. One is the arrangement of the room. According to John G. Demaray, in *Shakespeare and the Spectacles of Strangeness:* The Tempest *and the Transformation of Renaissance Theatrical Forms* (Pittsburgh: Duquesne University Press, 1998, pages 76–77):

By Whitehall staging custom the Cell and Court of
Prospero [on a raised stage at one end of the long
banqueting hall] would have been placed at the same
height as the uplifted state seat of James I and his
court at the hall's opposite end. Only from the King's
perspective would Prospero's Cell and the rest of the
stage setting have been seen in perfect perspective.

The play, then, would have unfolded between the seat of
Prospero on stage and the contrasting seat of James in
the hall proper, with action flowing forward and
downward from the stage to the central, green-carpeted
area in intimate proximity to the king and spectators.

To suppose that this play was only *ever* performed
twice is impractical. It has long been believed that the
play was very likely performed at the Blackfriars, the
indoor playhouse acquired by Shakespeare and his
partners in the King's Men in 1608. At the Blackfriars Theatre, as at Whitehall, would be available scenic
effects to enhance the banquet scene (Act III, Scene
3) and the wedding masque (Act IV, Scene 1), including the ability to fly characters or scenery in on ropes
and the use of elaborate traps or "quaint device[s]" (as
the stage directions indicate) to make the banquet disappear. The Globe would certainly have had a trap
and possibly limited abilities to lower characters on
stage by means of mechanical devices. Although no
records of performances of *The Tempest* at either the
Blackfriars or the Globe exist, we are on relatively safe
ground in assuming that the play was performed at
one or both of these venues, if for no other reason than
as part of the preparation of performing the play first
for the King in 1611 and a year later for Princess Elizabeth and Frederick, The Elector Palatine.

That *The Tempest* was performed twice at court
suggests that it was highly regarded in its own day.
Furthermore, the prestigious position the printed text
was allowed when Shakespeare's business partners,
John Heminges and Henry Condell, came to supervise the publication of the First Folio in 1623 also
suggests that this play had much to recommend it.

Undoubtedly, *The Tempest* continued to be performed by Shakespeare's company after his retirement to Stratford-on-Avon shortly after he wrote it,
and even after his death a few years later, in 1616.
Later still, however, the play was adapted for performance. John Dryden and William Davenant in
1667 altered the play by adding characters and giving it an alternate title: *The Tempest, or The*
Enchanted Isle. The Davenant-Dryden adaptation
was enormously popular and frequently revived.
Increasingly elaborate stage machinery was used to
produce flying spirits and spectacular effects far
beyond those detailed in Shakespeare's original text.

It was not until 1838 that William Charles
Macready staged a version of the play that, at least
in terms of the text, was closer to that of Shakespeare's original than had been put on stage in over
200 years. Although the text of Shakespeare's play
may have gone somewhat underground as far as the
stage is concerned during this period, as a play to be
read and studied, *The Tempest* continued to be
explored.

The Tempest has been highly regarded by most
critics almost from the moment it was written.
Shakespeare's contemporary Ben Jonson, who was
highly critical of the general disregard in Shakespeare's plays for observing the Aristotelian unity of
time, place, and action, should have been impressed
with Shakespeare's strict adherence to these precepts
in *The Tempest*. Instead, Jonson displays characteristic contempt by referring slyly to Shakespeare's late
plays — and probably specifically to Shakespeare's
"servant-monster" Caliban — in the introduction to
his own play *Bartholomew Fair*:

If there be never a servant-monster i' the Fair, who can
help it? he [the author, Ben Jonson] says; nor a nest of
antics? He is loath to make Nature afraid in his plays,
like those that beget Tales, Tempests, and such like
drolleries to mix his head with other men's heels. . . .

Subsequent critics have found much to praise in the play. Some have been concerned with arguing that the text we have is altered from an earlier version of the play. Specifically, this argument has to do with the early performances of the play and the suggestion that the betrothal masque in Act IV was added specifically for the second recorded performance in 1612–1613. That this is so is certainly possible but in no way absolutely certain. The significance of the marriage as a vehicle for redemption and reconciliation, central themes in the play, is too neatly incorporated into the overall fabric of the play to make such a conjecture altogether believable, however.

A longstanding tradition has sought to read Prospero as a semi-autobiographical representation of Shakespeare himself. This is tempting, especially given Prospero's pronouncement near the end of the play that following its work he will break his staff, drown his book, and allow every third thought he has to be of his grave — a pronouncement that came only a few months before Shakespeare's retirement from playwriting. This notion is a somewhat fanciful one, however, and one that most critics today approach with a great deal of skepticism. Certainly it is true that Prospero is a parallel figure for a playwright or director of entertainment in general, and in this regard the character is part of a long tradition in Shakespeare that embeds commentary on the theatre and theatrical practice into the plays themselves. If we look to read Prospero as the representation of an actual person, we would be better served to understand him as a figuration of King James (see the commentaries on Act I, Scene 2; Act V, Scene 1; and the Epilogue, for more discussion of this).

More recent criticism of *The Tempest* has focused on the issues of colonialism that are at work in the play. The affinities in the play with the wreck of the *Sea-Adventure*, as well as the play's date of composition and performance, ally it with the colonization of the New World. In colonial readings of the play, Prospero is seen as the European colonizer and Ariel and Caliban as the native people who are subjected to his will. Issues of colonialism and of power are undeniably at work in the play; however, to suggest that this is the main concern of the play and to throw all of our focus as readers and audience members onto the relationship between Caliban and Prospero and/or Prospero and Ariel, and to look to the play as either a simple endorsement or condemnation of colonialism, is misguided. Better still is to read the actions of Prospero as a colonist and Caliban and Ariel as his subjects in the larger

A modern stage production of The Tempest.
Henrietta Butler/PAL

context of the division between Art as it is perceived by the so-called civilized Old World and its interaction with Nature and the New World (that is, the over-simplified assumption that the sophistication of the Old World and its artfulness is inherently superior to the rawness of Nature and the New World.) This relationship and its complex treatment in the play is given fuller discussion in "Key themes of *The Tempest*". In understanding the conflicts between Prospero and Caliban as part of a larger statement on the clashes of an Old World order and a New World order, we can better look at Shakespeare's play as a whole and consider how Stephano's treatment as a potential colonizer of the New World and master to Caliban fits in with Prospero's actions. Likewise, the parallel plots hatched by Caliban to overthrow Prospero and the plot devised by Antonio and Sebastian to supplant Alonso can be viewed in this larger context of political struggle as a product of civilization and the workings of Man versus Nature.

Synopsis of the play

The Tempest opens with a dramatic scene of a ship caught in a violent and tempestuous storm. At the scene's conclusion, the sailors and noblemen onboard the ship are nearly all convinced that their cause is lost and their deaths by drowning unavoidable.

We learn immediately in the next scene that this is not the case. Prospero, a magician and formerly the Duke of Milan, has created the storm and used it to make the men on the ship believe that they have wrecked. Instead, he has ensured that all survive without a scratch. Prospero tells his daughter, Miranda, the background story that has resulted in their coming to this desert island twelve years before. His story is one of political intrigue and betrayal.

Prospero's magical servant, Ariel, is the agent who makes the storm and supposed shipwreck happen, and further causes the travelers to be separated into three groups. Ariel leaves the sailors locked

inside the ship. Washed ashore on a remote part of the island are Alonso, the King of Naples; Sebastian, his brother; Antonio, Prospero's brother who has supplanted him as Duke of Milan; Gonzalo, a noble lord who was kind to Prospero in days long past; and a handful of other lords or courtiers. The King and his party believe that Ferdinand, King Alonso's son, is drowned, because he did not wash ashore with them. Gonzalo remains hopeful that Ferdinand did not drown and encourages the others to search for him. Ferdinand is deposited on his own in another part of the island, and in still another part of the island Ariel leaves Stephano, the King's drunken butler, and Trinculo, the court jester.

Ferdinand believes that his father is drowned, but his grief is quickly removed by meeting and falling immediately in love with Prospero's daughter, Miranda. She, too, is impressed with him — as Prospero had hoped she would be. Prospero's overarching plan to regain political power is strengthened by a dynastic marriage between the ruling families of Naples (Alonso, Ferdinand) and Milan (Prospero, Miranda). Prospero requires that Ferdinand prove his worthiness to marry Miranda by putting the prince to work hauling firewood.

Meanwhile, as the King and his party search unsuccessfully for Ferdinand, Stephano (who is washed ashore on a barrel of wine) meets up with his friend Trinculo, and together they encounter Caliban, the "savage and deformed" monster who serves Prospero in a variety of menial ways. Stephano and Trinculo give Caliban his first taste of liquor, an experience so magical for him that he proclaims Stephano a god and convinces the drunken butler and tipsy jester to join him in rebellion against Prospero.

As they wander about the island in search of Ferdinand, the King and his party grow increasingly frustrated, tired, and hungry. At one point, when they fall asleep from their weariness, Antonio (Prospero's brother) and Sebastian (King Alonso's brother) devise a plot to kill the King and replace him with

Sebastian. Ariel prevents this from happening and later, as the group wanders further, presents a tantalizing banquet before them only to cause it to disappear in dramatic fashion. Ariel appears in the form of a harpy, sent to remind Antonio, Sebastian, and Alonso that they are "three men of sin." Reminded of their betrayal of Prospero, Ariel leaves them to wander closer still to Prospero himself and the wronged Duke of Milan's long-awaited revenge.

Ferdinand passes Prospero's trials successfully and is rewarded with the promise of marriage to Miranda. He is several times reminded sternly by Prospero not to destroy Miranda's virgin purity prior to the actual marriage, however. As a further reward, Prospero devises a masque in celebration of marriage to be presented before Miranda and Ferdinand. In the masque, three goddesses appear and sing of harmony in nature and the triumph of forgiveness, fertility, and regeneration. The masque dissolves suddenly, however, when Prospero remembers the plot hatched by Caliban and his drunken friends.

Caliban, Stephano, and Trinculo are led by Ariel's music to Prospero's cell and there they are shown fancy costumes of gold, silver, and expensive cloth. Seeing this "trumpery," Stephano and Trinculo immediately forget about the plot to murder Prospero and take over the island. Prospero unleashes his hell hounds on the three of them and contains them through his magic powers until it is time to address them properly for their murderous plans.

In the final scene of the play, all of Prospero's enemies lie within his power and stand in perfect position to be punished and possibly destroyed by him. Ariel suggests that Prospero would have pity on his enemies were he but to see the state of sadness and grief to which all of these events have led "the good old lord Gonzalo." Prospero agrees and resolves to forgive his enemies rather than destroy them. All of the groups that Ariel separated through the opening tempest are reunited in the final moments of the play: Alonso, repentant for his part in overthrowing Prospero twelve years ago is forgiven; Ferdinand is revealed to be alive and promised in marriage to Prospero's daughter, information that brings Alonso great joy; the sailors are set free from the ship and reunited with the King and his company; Stephano, Trinculo, and Caliban — smelling of drink and a wrong turn through a foul swamp — are likewise reunited with the others and voice their repentance for their stupidity and excessive drunkenness.

Prospero welcomes the court party and the sailors into his humble home and then turns to congratulate and thank Ariel for enacting all his magical commands. Prospero promises the freedom Ariel has long awaited, conditional only on Ariel seeing Prospero and all the others (except, probably, for Caliban) safely back to Italy.

Prospero concludes the play by speaking an Epilogue that begs the audience for applause and forgiveness.

Key themes of *The Tempest*

The Tempest is a play about education and awareness. It conveys the idea that, through enhanced awareness of ourselves and our surroundings, we can come to seek forgiveness for our own inadequacies and to forgive others for theirs. This seemingly straightforward theme is given complex presentation in the play and is showcased in a variety of symbolic and metaphorical ways. These various presentations lead to a sense of contributory sub-themes, all of which ultimately support the larger project of education that leads to redemption.

Perhaps principal among the sub-themes at work in the play is the interplay between Art and Nature. The presentation of the interaction between these two forces (somewhat violently) was of major concern to Shakespeare throughout his career and reached an ever-increasing refinement of expression in his final plays. In *The Tempest*, as elsewhere,

Shakespeare explores the contradictions in what many of his age would have seen as a relatively straightforward, clear-cut relationship, in which Art, or that which is manmade, is everything good (sophisticated, controlled, civilized, and precise), whereas Nature, although abundant as the source material that Art can improve upon, is ultimately flawed and imperfect. That this view was Shakespeare's is not necessarily as easily asserted. Frequently in Shakespeare's plays, he exposes the artful or artificial as corrupt and the natural as naturally superior to anything touched by or created by Man. In his presentation of Caliban, we see Shakespeare exploring the rich complexity of this theme.

Caliban is variously described as a "monster," a "moon-calf," a "devil," a "freckled whelp, hag born," "earth," and "natural." He is labeled in the *dramatis personae* as a "savage and deformed slave." Caliban is Nature in all its rawness and mystery. Prospero says that he is corrupt and one who is more moved by stripes or beating than kindness, that he is "A devil, a born devil, on whose nature / Nurture can never stick" (IV.1.188–189).

We learn in the opening scene, from Caliban's own report as well as through Prospero and Miranda, that when Prospero first arrived on the island he treated Caliban with kindness and lodged him in his own home. Prospero and Miranda taught him to speak, and he in turn showed them where to find fresh water and edible plants, and how to trap animals and birds worth eating. But Caliban turned on them, seeking to rape Miranda in order to have "peopled else / This isle with Calibans" (I.2.352–353). He reverted to his devilish nature, corrupting even language; his only profit on learning to speak, he claims, is that he can curse.

To see Caliban as darkness and evil personified is too easy, however. For all his claims that his only benefit from learning language is the ability to curse, it is Caliban who provides the most lyrical descriptions of the play and its mysterious, musical magic.

Just as Nature cannot be reduced to all things base and worthwhile only if enhanced by Art, so Art and civilization are questioned as themselves flawed in *The Tempest*. As representatives — albeit low-class ones — of civilization, Stephano and Trinculo do more to corrupt Caliban than to improve him. Stephano exemplifies the dreams of crass, capitalistic civilization when he imagines how much money he can get by transporting Caliban as an oddity of Nature and the New World back to Europe.

Similarly, the urbane and sophisticated courtiers prove significantly poor examples of humanity, Gonzalo excepted. Antonio and Sebastian laugh in their sophistication at the supposed mistakes Gonzalo makes in labeling Dido a "widow" and with suggesting that Carthage and Tunis, are one and the same city. Antonio and Sebastian's knowledge is representative of civilized, artful learning writ large and, on the point of Carthage and Tunis, they are technically correct; they are morally flawed, however. Antonio proves that his greatest skill in language is convincing himself and others to commit the sin of fratricide and to give his ambition and political desire as free a reign as Caliban would give to his sexual desires. Something is indeed rotten in the state of Art in this play, and it is through a reassessment of Nature that a better Art can be devised and a genuine sense of redemption and regeneration achieved.

What is achieved in *The Tempest* is a marriage of Art and Nature that corrects the imperfections of both in a new creation. The Masque in Act IV, a celebration of marriage, also symbolizes this sub-theme. In their songs, the goddesses sing of conflict among the gods and the resulting conflict in Nature that arises: Winter kills all vegetable life on Earth as a result of Ceres' anger at the abduction and rape of her daughter, Proserpine. Juno convinces her to forgive, however, to restore Springtime to the Earth and to allow for rebirth and regeneration.

Juno, the marriage goddess, oversees a reconciliatory marriage of the elements. Earth is reconciled with heaven, land with sea, hot with cold, wet with dry, spring with harvest. What Ceres and Juno also achieve is a sense of temperance, or moderation. *Temperance*, a synonym for *temperate*, can also be used to describe the island both in terms of climate and for the fruitfulness or fertility that goes along with a temperate climate. The island is a space for regeneration and discovery, a place where the marriage of disparate elements — like Art and Nature, rage and forgiveness, grief and hope — can come together.

The play's overall thematic movement of division leading to eventual reconciliation can also be seen in the progress of social division or conflict as represented by the arguments between the sailors and the court party in the play's opening scene and their eventual reunion and reconciliation in the final scene. This is another metaphorical marriage of two conflicting elements that, when conjoined, brings about a new whole greater than the sum of its parts.

Marriage becomes a powerful symbol in the play and represents just this sort of combination of conflicting elements; through harmonious combinations, peace, reconciliation, and redemption are achieved. Certainly, this is the case in the actual (anticipated) marriage of Ferdinand and Miranda that concludes the play and the Masque celebrations. In the union of Ferdinand and Miranda, the sins of their fathers are forgiven: The sins of Alonso (his alliance with Antonio to supplant Prospero) and Prospero (his Lear-like desire to cast off the responsibility of government and enjoy only its spoils) are forgiven and redeemed by their children being joined in a union that will bring peace and prosperity to the future.

Prospero is not only forgiven, he learns to forgive and proves the wise schoolteacher of virtually every character in the play. He exposes Alonso, Antonio, and Sebastian for their sinfulness and wicked ways. When Alonso proves repentant, he is forgiven and redeemed. Antonio and Sebastian are not so clearly repentant of their ways, and their forgiveness and redemption, consequently, far less certain. Ferdinand and Miranda are taught patience, perseverance, and obedience and rewarded with each other as marriage partners. Caliban, Stephano, and Trinculo are taught the errors of a comic subversion of the ambition characterized by Antonio and Sebastian — the unnatural ambition that twelve years before put into motion the events necessary for this story to come into being. In repenting the errors of their ways, they too are forgiven. Ariel is taught a patience in servitude, similar to that of Ferdinand and Miranda, and is rewarded with freedom. The neatness of all this is summarized by Gonzalo near the end of the play:

> Was Milan thrust from Milan, that his issue
>   Should become Kings of Naples? O, rejoice
>   Beyond a common joy! and set down
>   With gold on lasting pillars: in one voyage
>   Did Claribel her husband find at Tunis,
>   And Ferdinand, her brother, found a wife
>   Where he himself was lost, Prospero his dukedom
>   In a poor isle, and all of us ourselves
>   When no man was his own. (V.1.205–213)

Finally, in the Epilogue to the play, the actor playing Prospero steps partially out of his role and asks forgiveness of the audience. The theme is carried from out of the play and into the playhouse where it is being performed. Prospero reminds us of our own imperfections in his Epilogue, reworking the words of the Lord's Prayer ("Forgive us our trespasses as we forgive those who trespass against us") to become, "As you from crimes would pardoned be, let your indulgence set me free." We are, all of us, imperfect, and this play reminds us of that. But when we come to learn this and repent of it, we can and will be remade into something better.

CHARACTERS IN THE PLAY

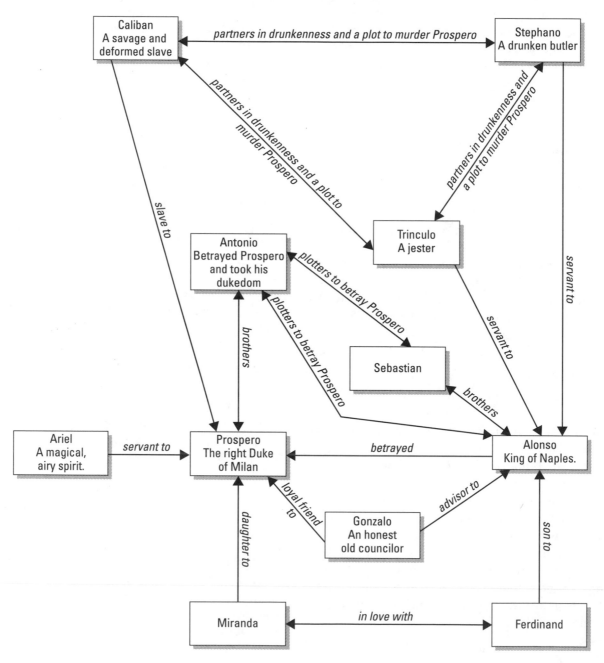

THE TEMPEST

ACT I

Prospero *They are both in either's powers; but this swift business*
I must uneasy make, lest too light winning
Make the prize light.

Act I, Scene 1

On board a storm-tossed ship at sea, sailors must battle against not only the elements but also the interference of King Alonso and his attendants. As the storm worsens, nearly everyone aboard the vessel — from the King to the lowliest sailor — is convinced that they are doomed to shipwreck and to death.

ACT I, SCENE 1
[A ship at sea.]

A tempestuous noise of thunder and lightning heard. Enter a
SHIPMASTER *and a* BOATSWAIN.

Master Boatswain!

Boatswain Here, master. What cheer?

Master Good, speak to th' mariners; fall to't
yarely, or we run ourselves aground. Bestir, bestir!

Enter MARINERS.

Boatswain Heigh, my hearts! Cheerly, cheerly,　　　　5
my hearts! Yare, yare! Take in the topsail! Tend
to th' master's whistle! Blow till thou burst thy
wind, if room enough!

Enter ALONSO, SEBASTIAN, ANTONIO, FERDINAND,
GONZALO, *and* Others.

Alonso Good boatswain, have care. Where's the
master? Play the men.　　　　　　　　　　　　10

Boatswain I pray now, keep below.

Antonio Where is the master, bos'n?

Boatswain Do you not hear him? You mar our
labor. Keep your cabins: you do assist the storm.

Gonzalo Nay, good, be patient.　　　　　　　　15

Boatswain When the sea is. Hence! What cares
these roarers for the name of king? To cabin!
Silence! Trouble us not!

Gonzalo Good, yet remember whom thou hast
aboard.　　　　　　　　　　　　　　　　　20

Boatswain None that I more love than myself.
You are a councilor: if you can command these
elements to silence and work the peace of the

NOTES

1.   *Boatswain:* (BO-sun) See line 12. The first mate.

3.   *Good:* good man or fellow.
4.   *yarely:* quickly, smartly.

5.   *Cheerly:* cheerfully, with a positive attitude.

7.   *Blow . . . :* addressed to the storm.

10.   *Play:* Attend to the men; keep them on task.

12.   *bos'n:* (bo'-sun) See line 1.

15.   *good:* man, understood as at line 3.

16.   *What cares:* a common usage in Early Modern English of the singular form of the verb with a plural subject.

17.   *roarers:* roaring winds and thunder claps.

present, we will not hand a rope more; use your authority. If you cannot, give thanks you have lived   25
so long, and make yourself ready in your cabin
for the mischance of the hour, if it so hap. —
Cheerily, good hearts! — Out of our way, I say. *Exeunt*

Gonzalo I have great comfort from this fellow:
methinks he hath no drowning mark upon him; his   30
complexion is perfect gallows. Stand fast, good Fate,
to his hanging! Make the rope of his destiny our
cable, for our own doth little advantage. If he be
not born to be hanged, our case is miserable. *Exit*

Enter BOATSWAIN.

Boatswain Down with the topmast! Yare! Lower,   35
lower! Bring her to try with main-course! (*A cry within.*)
A plague upon this howling! They are
louder than the weather or our office.

Enter SEBASTIAN, ANTONIO, *and* GONZALO.
Yet again? What do you here? Shall we give o'er
and drown? Have you a mind to sink?   40

Sebastian A'pox o' your throat, you bawling, blasphemous, incharitable dog!

Boatswain Work you, then.

Antonio Hang, cur, hang, you whoreson, insolent
noisemaker! We are less afraid to be drowned than   45
thou art.

Gonzalo I'll warrant him for drowning, though the
ship were no stronger than a nutshell and as leaky
as an unstanched wench.

Boatswain Lay her ahold, ahold! Set her two   50
courses off to sea again. Lay her off!

Enter MARINERS *wet.*

Mariners All lost! To prayers, to prayers! All lost!

Exeunt

Boatswain What, must our mouths be cold?

Gonzalo The King and Prince at prayers, let's
assist them,

---

24.   *hand:* i.e., handle.

26.   *make . . . ready:* prepare yourself — physically and spiritually — for death.

28.   *Cheerily, good hearts!:* the boatswain addresses this to the sailors, and turns, with his next phrase, to brush the court party aside.

31.   *complexion:* his face, as an indication of character or temperament.

  Stand fast . . . hanging!: an allusion to the proverb "Who's born to be hanged will never drown."

36.   *to try:* to lie hull-to or hove-to; lower the mainsail and stand nearly stationary.

  main-course: mainsail.

38.   *louder than . . . office:* i.e., the "howling" of the passengers makes more noise than either the weather or the sailors at their work ("office").

39.   *Shall we give o'er:* i.e., shall we give up, because of your interference, and drown?

47.   *I'll warrant . . . drowning:* I'll guarantee that he won't drown.

49.   *unstanched:* loose.

51.   *Lay her ahold:* i.e., a-hull, or hove-to. The boatswain immediately reverses this order ("Off to sea again!") when he sees there is no room to lie-to. The nautically minded Early Modern audience would understand the crisis implied in this reversal. The sea-drenched mariners who now enter confirm the danger.

52.   *cold:* cold without the opportunity to enjoy a final drink.

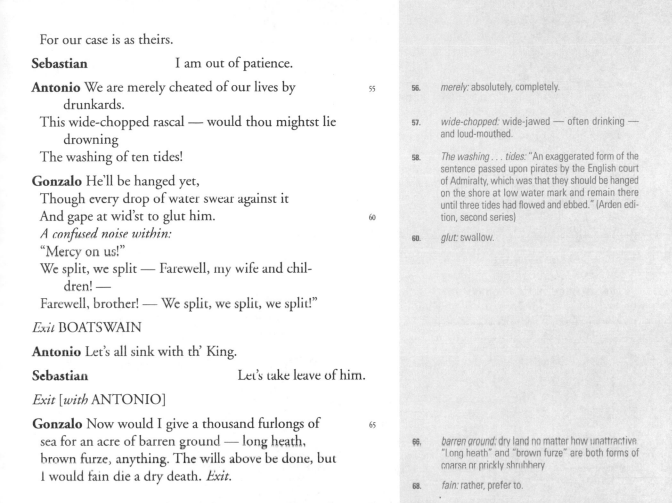

For our case is as theirs.

Sebastian　　　　　　　I am out of patience.

Antonio We are merely cheated of our lives by 　　　55
　　drunkards.
　This wide-chopped rascal — would thou mightst lie
　　drowning
　The washing of ten tides!

Gonzalo He'll be hanged yet,
　Though every drop of water swear against it
　And gape at wid'st to glut him. 　　　　　　　　60
　A confused noise within:
　"Mercy on us!"
　We split, we split — Farewell, my wife and chil-
　　dren! —
　Farewell, brother! — We split, we split, we split!"

Exit BOATSWAIN

Antonio Let's all sink with th' King.

Sebastian　　　　　　　Let's take leave of him.

Exit [*with* ANTONIO]

Gonzalo Now would I give a thousand furlongs of 　　65
　sea for an acre of barren ground — long heath,
　brown furze, anything. The wills above be done, but
　I would fain die a dry death. *Exit.*

56. *merely:* absolutely, completely.

57. *wide-chopped:* wide-jawed — often drinking — and loud-mouthed.

58. *The washing . . . tides:* "An exaggerated form of the sentence passed upon pirates by the English court of Admiralty, which was that they should be hanged on the shore at low water mark and remain there until three tides had flowed and ebbed." (Arden edition, second series)

60. *glut:* swallow.

66. *barren ground:* dry land no matter how unattractive. "Long heath" and "brown furze" are both forms of coarse or prickly shrubbery.

68. *fain:* rather, prefer to.

COMMENTARY

Shakespeare uses this short opening scene to immediately grab his audience and yank them into his play. The setting is a ship at sea being violently tossed about by the sea-storm that, in part, gives the play its name. Although there is no direct evidence proving that *The Tempest* was performed at the Globe (the famous open-air, public amphitheatre-style playing house owned by Shakespeare and his partners in the King's Men), the power of this noisy scene to start the play in a vivid, dramatic fashion is certainly a trick of the trade Shakespeare developed by writing plays to be performed at the Globe, a theatre with an estimated seating capacity of over 3,000.

This opening is a masterful one, which comes as no surprise given the late point in Shakespeare's career when this play was written. In a little less than 100 lines, Shakespeare creates two conflicts — Man against Nature and Man against Man (showing conflict between differing social and economic classes and manners) — two of the play's major themes.

Important information is also imparted here. Elements of character emerge as we are first introduced to the King and the court party (attendants of the king — lords, dukes, earls, barons, and knights were known as the *court*). The King is gracious but clearly not in control in this scene. Among the humans, the most powerful and controlling character in Scene 1 is the Boatswain (pronounced BO-sun). The manner in which the different characters deal with the threat of death by shipwreck begins to suggest something of their inner character. The court party (Gonzalo, Antonio, and Sebastian) are out of place on the ship's decks during a storm. Antonio and Sebastian only make this worse by insulting and curs-

"Lay her a hold, a hold!" (I.1.49). The leeboard is a rudder-like attachment that might aid with the sort of maneuver that the Boatswain calls for here, which is, in effect, to make the ship stand still.

ing the sailors ("A pox . . . ," "hang cur," and so on), especially the no-nonsense Boatswain.

These men, even the Boatswain, who operates as though he has seen this type of storm before (and he probably has) are afraid. The Boatswain seeks comfort in drink. Antonio and Sebastian grow upset, and attempt to shout insulting commands at the sailors. No doubt their words are largely swallowed by the storm. Gonzalo is humorously philosophical, however. He concludes that the Boatswain has too much of the criminal about him to die in a shipwreck; the Boatswain, in Gonzalo's estimation, is destined to die by hanging on dry land.

"Down with the topmast! Yare!" (I.1.34). The play opens dramatically, with a group of sailors battling valiantly against a frightening storm. Their ship is most likely not a large one, making the danger all the greater.
Tate Gallery, London/A.K.G., Berlin/SuperStock

Act I, Scene 2

Prospero recounts for his daughter, Miranda, the series of events that led them to their desert island home some twelve years before, including Prospero's betrayal by his brother, Antonio. Ariel, the airy spirit who carries out Prospero's magical commands, appears and recounts the work performed in the supposed shipwreck of the opening scene and reveals instead that the ship and all her passengers are safe. Caliban, Prospero's earthy slave, is also presented, and a background of betrayal and distrust — between Caliban and Prospero, between Prospero and Ariel — is revealed. Ferdinand, King Alonso's son, is led in by Ariel's music and, according to Prospero's plan, Ferdinand and Miranda meet and fall immediately in love.

ACT I, SCENE 2
[Before Prospero's cell]

Enter PROSPERO *and* MIRANDA.

Miranda If by your art, my dearest father, you have
Put the wild waters in this roar, allay them.
The sky, it seems, would pour down stinking pitch
But that the sea, mounting to th' welkin's cheek,
Dashes the fire out. O, I have suffered   5
With those that I saw suffer! a brave vessel
(Who had no doubt some noble creature in her)
Dashed all to pieces! O, the cry did knock
Against my very heart! Poor souls, they perished!
Had I been any god of power, I would   10
Have sunk the sea within the earth or ere
It should the good ship so have swallowed and
The fraughting souls within her.

Prospero   Be collected.
No more amazement. Tell your piteous heart
There's no harm done.   15

Miranda   O, woe the day!

Prospero   No harm.
I have done nothing but in care of thee,
Of thee my dear one, thee my daughter, who

NOTES

SD.   *Cell:* used here in the Early Modern sense of a small room, or dwelling, as in a monk's cell; on the stage Prospero's cell would be represented by the curtained inner stage. Prospero and Miranda's home is notably simple, "full poor" in Prospero's own description.

1.   *art:* here, the art of magic.

2.   *allay:* relieve or calm.

3.   *pitch:* tar.

4.   *welkin's cheek:* face of the sky.

6.   *brave:* fine in appearance (as elsewhere in Shakespeare).

11.   *or ere:* before.

13.   *fraughting:* forming the freight or cargo but also with a suggestion of frightened.

      collected: calm, composed.

14.   *piteous:* full of pity.

Art ignorant of what thou art, naught knowing
Of whence I am; nor that I am more better
Than Prospero, master of a full poor cell,   20
And thy no greater father.

Miranda   More to know
Did never meddle with my thoughts.

Prospero   'Tis time
I should inform thee farther. Lend thy hand
And pluck my magic garment from me. So,
Lie there, my art. Wipe thou thine eyes; have   25
    comfort.
The direful spectacle of the wrack, which touched
The very virtue of compassion in thee,
I have with such provision in mine art
So safely ordered that there is no soul-
No, not so much perdition as an hair   30
Betid to any creature in the vessel
Which thou heard'st cry, which thou saw'st sink. Sit
    down;
For thou must now know farther.

Miranda   You have often
Begun to tell me what I am; but stopped
And left me to a bootless inquisition,   35
Concluding, "Stay: not yet."

Prospero   The hour's now come;
The very minute bids thee ope thine ear.
Obey, and be attentive. Canst thou remember
A time before we came unto this cell?
I do not think thou canst, for then thou wast not   40
Out three years old.

Miranda   Certainly, sir I can.

Prospero By what? By any other house or person?
Of any thing the image tell me that
Hath kept with thy remembrance.

Miranda   'Tis far off,
And rather like a dream than an assurance   45
That my remembrance warrants. Had I not
Four or five women once that tended me?

19. *more better:* a double comparative, common in Early Modern English.

22. *meddle with:* come into.

25. *my art:* i.e., his magic robe, which he here takes off.

27. *the very virtue:* the innermost essence.

28. *provision:* both steps to provide and positive vision or foresight.

30. *perdition:* loss.

31. *Betid:* happened.

35. *bootless inquisition:* unanswered questions.

41. *not / Out:* not yet, not more than.

43. *Of any . . . me:* i.e., describe anything to me that you can remember.

46. *dream . . . remembrance warrants:* more like a dream than a clear memory.

Prospero Thou hadst, and more, Miranda. But how
    is it
That this lives in thy mind? What seest thou else
In the dark backward and abysm of time?   50
If thou rememb'rest aught ere thou cam'st here,
How thou cam'st here thou mayst.

Miranda   But that I do not.

Prospero Twelve year since, Miranda, twelve year
    since,
Thy father was the Duke of Milan and
A prince of power.   55

Miranda   Sir, are not you my father?

Prospero Thy mother was a piece of virtue, and
She said thou wast my daughter; and thy father
Was Duke of Milan, and his only heir
A princess — no worse issued.

Miranda   O the heavens!
What foul play had we that we came from thence?   60
Or blessed was't we did?

Prospero   Both, both, my girl!
By foul play, as thou say'st, were we heaved thence,
But blessedly holp hither.

Miranda   O, my heart bleeds
To think o' th' teen that I have turned you to,
Which is from my remembrance! Please you, farther.   65

Prospero My brother and thy uncle, called
    Antonio —
I pray thee mark me — that a brother should
Be so perfidious! — he whom next thyself
Of all the world I loved, and to him put
The manage of my state, as at that time   70
Through all the signories it was the first
And Prospero the prime duke, being so reputed
In dignity, and for the liberal arts
Without a parallel; those being all my study,
The government I cast upon my brother   75
And to my state grew stranger, being transported

50.   *backward and abysm:* past and abyss (vast emptiness).

51.   *aught ere:* anything from before.

53.   *twelve years:* Miranda is approximately 15 years old since she was not quite 3 when banished to the island.

56.   *piece:* perfect specimen or masterpiece

59.   *no worse issued:* of no lower parentage.

63.   *holp:* helped.

64.   *teen:* pain, trouble, or anxiety.

      turned you to: reminded you of.

65.   *from my remembrance:* not in my memory.

66 ff.   The jumbled nature of Prospero's speaking suggests the emotional power this story holds for him even after twelve years.

69–70.   *and to him . . . state:* and gave him the control of my state.

71.   *signories:* Italian states (those subject to a signior, or lord).

76.   *And to . . . stranger:* i.e., withdrew from my position as head of the state.

And rapt in secret studies. Thy false uncle —
Dost thou attend me?

Miranda   Sir, most heedfully.

Prospero Being once perfected how to grant suits,
How to deny them, who t' advance, and who   80
To trash for over-topping, new-created
The creatures that were mine, I say, or changed 'em,
Or else new-formed 'em; having both the key
Of officer and office, set all hearts i' th' state
To what tune pleased his ear, that now he was   85
The ivy which had hid my princely trunk
And sucked my verdure out on't. Thou attend'st
    not?

Miranda O, good sir, I do.

Prospero   I pray thee mark me.
I thus neglecting worldly ends, all dedicated
To closeness, and the bettering of my mind   90
With that which, but by being so retired,
O'er-prized all popular rate, in my false brother
Awaked an evil nature, and my trust,
Like a good parent, did beget of him
A falsehood in its contrary as great   95
As my trust was, which had indeed no limit,
A confidence sans bound. He being thus lorded
Not only with what my revenue yielded
But what my power might else exact, like one
Who having unto truth, by telling of it,   100
Made such a sinner of his memory
To credit his own lie, he did believe
He was indeed the Duke, out o' th' substitution
And executing th' outward face of royalty
With all prerogative. Hence his ambition growing —   105
Dost thou hear?

Miranda   Your tale, sir, would cure deafness.

Prospero To have no screen between this part he
    played
And him he played it for, he needs will be
Absolute Milan. Me (poor man) my library

---

77.   *rapt:* wrapped up in or absorbed.

79.   *perfected:* grown skillful in.

81.   *trash for over-topping:* check for being too bold.

       new-created: i.e., transformed my supporters into his.

83.   *key:* the word is suggested by key of office, then leads, by its musical association, to "tune."

87.   *verdure:* vitality, health; the ivy is a parasite.

89–97. "The fact of my retirement, in which I neglected worldly affairs and dedicated myself to secret studies of a kind beyond the understanding and esteem of the people, brought out a bad side of my brother's nature. Consequently the great, indeed boundless, trust I placed in him gave rise to a disloyalty equally great on his part, just as it sometimes happens that a father distinguished for virtue has a vicious son" (Arden edition, second series).

90.   *closeness:* secret (studies).

92.   *O'er-prized:* overvalued; i.e., was worth more to me than a good public opinion.

97.   *sans:* without.

       lorded: made lord of.

100–103. *Who having . . . Duke:* i.e., who, by often telling a lie, made his memory such a sinner against truth, that he came to believe the lie he told, that he was in fact the Duke.

103.   *out:* as a result.

107.   *To have . . . Milan:* i.e., in order to make himself the Duke in name as well as function.

109.   *Absolute Milan:* the Duke of Milan in every sense; Milan is pronounced throughout with the accent on the first syllable.

Was dukedom large enough. Of temporal royalties   110
He thinks me now incapable; confederates
(So dry he was for sway) with th' King of Naples
To give him annual tribute, do him homage,
Subject his coronet to his crown, and bend
The dukedom yet unbowed (alas, poor Milan!)   115
To most ignoble stooping.

Miranda   O the heavens!

Prospero Mark his condition, and th' event: then
      tell me
If this might be a brother.

Miranda   I should sin
To think but nobly of my grandmother.
Good wombs have borne bad sons.   120

Prospero   Now the condition.
This King of Naples, being an enemy
To me inveterate, hearkens my brother's suit;
Which was, that he, in lieu o' th' premises
Of homage and I know not how much tribute,
Should presently extirpate me and mine   125
Out of the dukedom and confer fair Milan,
With all the honors, on my brother. Whereon,
A treacherous army levied, one midnight
Fated to th' purpose, did Antonio open
The gates of Milan; and, i' th' dead of darkness,   130
The ministers for th' purpose hurried thence
Me and thy crying self.

Miranda   Alack, for pity!
not rememb'ring how I cried out then,
Will cry it o'er again; it is a hint
That wrings mine eyes to't.   135

Prospero   Hear a little further,
And then I'll bring thee to the present business
Which now's upon's; without the which this story
Were most impertinent.

Miranda   Wherefore did they not
That hour destroy us?

110. *temporal royalties:* the rule of temporary, material things (as opposed to intellectual studies).

111. *confederates:* joins with.

112. *dry:* thirsty, eager.

114. *his coronet . . . his crown:* the rule of Milan, the king-dom of Naples.

117. *condition:* agreement.

   event: outcome.

   might be a brother: i.e., was an act of brotherly kind-ness.

119. *but:* in any way other than.

123. *in lieu . . . premises:* i.e., in exchange for Antonio agreeing to pay homage and tribute (protection money), Alonso provides the military strength to remove Prospero.

125. *presently:* immediately.

129. *Fated:* dedicated.

131. *ministers:* agents.

134. *hint:* occasion.

135. *wrings:* forces.

138. *impertinent:* not to the purpose (opposite of "pertinent").

Prospero   Well demanded, wench.
My tale provokes that question. Dear, they durst   140
    not,
So dear the love my people bore me; nor set
A mark so bloody on the business; but
With colors fairer painted their foul ends.
In few, they hurried us aboard a bark,
Bore us some leagues to sea; where they prepared   145
A rotten carcass of a butt, not rigged,
Nor tackle, sail, nor mast; the very rats
Instinctively have quit it. There they hoist us,
To cry to th' sea that roared to us; to sigh
To th' winds, whose pity, sighing back again,   150
Did us but loving wrong.

Miranda   Alack, what trouble
Was I then to you!

Prospero   O, a cherubin
Thou wast that did preserve me! Thou didst smile,
Infused with a fortitude from heaven,
When I have decked the sea with drops full salt,   155
Under my burden groaned; which raised in me
An undergoing stomach, to bear up
Against what should ensue.

Miranda   How came we ashore?

Prospero By providence divine.
Some food we had, and some fresh water, that   160
A noble Neapolitan, Gonzalo,
Out of his charity, who being then appointed
Master of this design, did give us, with
Rich garments, linens, stuffs, and necessaries
Which since have steaded much. So, of his gentle-   165
    ness,
Knowing I loved my books, he furnished me
From mine own library with volumes that
I prize above my dukedom.

Miranda   Would I might
But ever see that man!

140.	*durst:* dared.
144.	*In few:* in brief.
	bark: ship
146.	*butt:* barrel, tub.
	rigged . . . mast: not fitted out with ropes, sail, or mast.
151.	*loving wrong:* nature is portrayed as an uncaring — not a consciously destructive — force.
152.	*cherubin:* an angel.
155.	*decked:* decorated.
	drops full salt: tears.
156.	*which:* Miranda's smile.
157.	*undergoing stomach:* enduring spirit.
162.	*Neapolitan:* person from Naples.
165.	*steaded much:* stood us in good stead, been very helpful.

Prospero   Now I arise.
Sit still, and hear the last of our sea-sorrow.   170
Here in this island we arrived; and here
Have I, thy schoolmaster, made thee more profit
Than other princess can, that have more time
For vainer hours, and tutors not so careful.

Miranda Heavens thank you for't! And now I pray   175
        you, sir, —
For still 'tis beating in my mind, — your reason
For raising this sea-storm?

Prospero   Know thus far forth.
By accident most strange, bountiful Fortune
(Now my dear lady) hath mine enemies
Brought to this shore; and by my prescience   180
I find my zenith doth depend upon
A most auspicious star, whose influence
If now I court not, but omit, my fortunes
Will ever after droop. Here cease more questions.
Thou art inclined to sleep. 'Tis a good dullness,   185
And give it way. I know thou canst not choose.

[MIRANDA *sleeps*]
Come away, servant, come! I am ready now.
Approach, my Ariel: come!

Enter ARIEL.

Ariel All hail, great master! Grave sir, hail! I
        come
To answer thy best pleasure; be't to fly,   190
To swim, to dive into the fire, to ride
On the curled clouds. To thy strong bidding task
Ariel and all his quality.

Prospero   Hast thou, spirit,
Performed to point the tempest that I bade thee?

Ariel To every article.   195
I boarded the King's ship: now on the beak,
Now in the waist, the deck, in every cabin,
I flamed amazement: sometime I'd divide
And burn in many places; on the topmast,

172. *schoolmaster . . . careful:* i.e., with Prospero as her teacher, Miranda has been given a superb education.

173. *princess:* plural understood.

178. *Fortune:* luck or chance, here personified as a woman, traditionally she is blindfolded and rewards and punishes not with reason but based on the random spinning of a wheel.

181. *my zenith:* the high point of my fortune.

182. *influence . . . omit:* i.e., I have fallen under a lucky star and need to take advantage of this as I may not get another chance.

185. *good dullness:* i.e., this desire to sleep is good.

187. *come away:* come here.

192. *task:* put to work

193. *quality:* those spirits like Ariel.

194. *to point:* in every detail.

196. *beak:* bow.

The yards and boresprit would I flame distinctly,   200
Then meet and join. Jove's lightnings, the precursors
O' th' dreadful thunderclaps, more momentary
And sight-outrunning were not. The fire and cracks
Of sulphurous roaring the most mighty Neptune
Seem to besiege and make his bold waves tremble;   205
Yea, his dread trident shake.

Prospero   My brave spirit!
Who was so firm, so constant, that this coil
Would not infect his reason?

Ariel   Not a soul
But felt a fever of the mad and played
Some tricks of desperation. All but mariners   210
Plunged in the foaming brine and quit the vessel;
Then all afire with me: the King's son, Ferdinand,
With hair up-staring (then like reeds, not hair),
Was the first man that leapt; cried, "Hell is empty,
And all the devils are here!"   215

Prospero   Why, that's my spirit!
But was not this nigh shore?

Ariel   Close by, my master.

Prospero But are they, Ariel, safe?

Ariel   Not a hair perished;
On their sustaining garments not a blemish,
But fresher than before; and as thou bad'st me,
In troops I have dispersed them 'bout the isle.   220
The King's son have I landed by himself,
Whom I left cooling of the air with sighs
In an odd angle of the isle, and sitting,
His arms in this sad knot.

Prospero   Of the King's ship
The mariners say how thou hast disposed,   225
And all the rest o' th' fleet.

Ariel   Safely in harbor
Is the King's ship; in the deep nook where once
Thou call'dst me up at midnight to fetch dew
From the still-vexed Bermoothes, there she's hid;

---

200. *boresprit:* bowsprit; the spar extending from the front of the ship.

flame distinctly: burn in several places. Probably also a reference to Ariel appearing as St. Elmo's Fire (see Commentary).

201. *Jove:* also Jupiter, the Roman name of the Greek god Zeus.

207. *coil:* turmoil, uproar.

208. *infect his reason:* drive him mad.

209. *of the mad:* such as the mad feel.

213. *up-staring:* standing straight up.

218. *sustaining:* keeping them afloat.

219. *bad'st:* commanded

224. *this sad knot:* Ariel demonstrates this posture.

229. *still-vexed Bermoothes:* the continually stormy Bermudas; the spelling is an approximation of the Spanish pronunciation of the islands' proper name, Bermudez.

The mariners all under hatches stowed,   230
Who, with a charm joined to their suff'red labor,
I have left asleep; and for the rest o' th' fleet,
Which I dispersed, they all have met again,
And are upon the Mediterranean flote
Bound sadly home for Naples,   235
Supposing that they saw the King's ship wracked
And his great person perish.

Prospero   Ariel, thy charge
Exactly is performed; but there's more work.
What is the time o' th' day?

Ariel   Past the mid season.

Prospero At least two glasses. The time 'twixt six   240
    and now
Must by us both be spent most preciously.

Ariel Is there more toil? Since thou dost give me pains,
Let me remember thee what thou hast promised,
Which is not yet performed me.

Prospero   How now? moody?
What is't thou canst demand?   245

Ariel   My liberty.

Prospero Before the time be out? No more!

Ariel   I prithee,
Remember I have done thee worthy service,
Told thee no lies, made no mistakings, served
Without or grudge or grumblings. Thou did promise
To bate me a full year.   250

Prospero   Dost thou forget
From what a torment I did free thee?

Ariel   No.

Prospero Thou dost; and think'st it much to tread
    the ooze
Of the salt deep,
To run upon the sharp wind of the North,
To do me business in the veins o' th' earth   255
When it is baked with frost.

231. *suff'red labor:* the work they have done.

234. *flote:* flood or sea.

239. *mid season:* noon.

240. *glasses:* hour-glasses.

242. *pains:* tasks, work

246. *time:* allotted term of service.

249. *or . . . or:* either . . . or.

250. *bate:* abate, shorten the term of my service.

255. *veins:* underground streams.

Ariel   I do not, sir.

Prospero Thou liest, malignant thing! Hast thou
    forgot
The foul witch Sycorax, who with age and envy
Was grown into a hoop? Hast thou forgot her?

Ariel No, sir.   260

Prospero   Thou hast. Where was she born?
    Speak! Tell me!

Ariel Sir, in Argier.

Prospero   O, was she so? I must
Once in a month recount what thou hast been,
Which thou forget'st. This damned witch Sycorax,
For mischiefs manifold, and sorceries terrible
To enter human hearing, from Argier,   265
Thou know'st, was banished. For one thing she did
They would not take her life. Is not this true?

Ariel Ay, sir.

Prospero This blue-eyed hag was hither brought
    with child
And here was left by th' sailors. Thou, my slave,   270
As thou report'st thyself, wast then her servant;
And, for thou wast a spirit too delicate
To act her earthy and abhorred commands,
Refusing her grand hests, she did confine thee,
By help of her more potent ministers,   275
And in her most unmitigable rage,
Into a cloven pine; within which rift
Imprisoned thou didst painfully remain
A dozen years; within which space she died
And left thee there, where thou didst vent thy groans   280
As fast as millwheels strike. Then was this island
(Save for the son that she did litter here,
A freckled whelp, hag-born) not honored with
A human shape.

Ariel   Yes, Caliban her son.

Prospero Dull thing, I say so: he, that Caliban   285
Whom now I keep in service. Thou best know'st

258. *Sycorax:* the name is usually explained as a combination of the Greek words for sow (sys) and raven (korax); there may also be a connection with the classical witch Circe, whom Sycorax resembles in various ways.

envy: hatred.

261. *Argier:* Algiers.

266. *one thing she did:* Sycorax was pregnant, and therefore exiled instead of executed.

273. *earthy:* of the earth, as opposed to spiritual, airy, or magical work.

274. *hests:* commands.

281. *millwheels:* the paddles of a river-powered millwheel.

286. *Thou:* Prospero changes subject from Caliban to a direct address of Ariel. "Thou" / "thee" is a familiar form of address as opposed to "you," which is more formal.

What torment I did find thee in: thy groans
Did make wolves howl and penetrate the breasts
Of ever-angry bears. It was a torment
To lay upon the damned, which Sycorax   290
Could not again undo. It was mine art,
When I arrived and heard thee, that made gape
The pine, and let thee out.

Ariel   I thank thee, master.

Prospero If thou more murmur'st, I will rend an
    oak
And peg thee in his knotty entrails till   295
Thou hast howled away twelve winters.

Ariel   Pardon, master.
I will be correspondent to command
And do my spriting gently.

Prospero   Do so; and after two days
I will discharge thee.

Ariel   That's my noble master!
What shall I do? Say what? What shall I do?   300

Prospero Go make thyself like a nymph o' th'
    sea.
Be subject.
To no sight but thine and mine; invisible
To every eyeball else. Go take this shape
And hither come in't. Go! Hence with diligence!

Exit [ARIEL.]
Awake, dear heart, awake! Thou hast slept well.   305
Awake!

Miranda   The strangeness of your story put
Heaviness in me.

Prospero   Shake it off. Come on.
We'll visit Caliban, my slave, who never
Yields us kind answer.

Miranda   'Tis a villain, sir,
I do not love to look on.   310

Prospero   But as 'tis,
We cannot miss him: he does make our fire,

297. *correspondent:* obedient.

298. *And do . . . gently:* and do my work as asked; i.e., graciously and without complaint.

307. *heaviness:* drowsiness.

311. *miss:* do without.

Fetch in our wood, and serves in offices
That profit us. What, ho! slave! Caliban!
Thou earth, thou! Speak!

Caliban [*within*]   There's wood enough within.

Prospero Come forth, I say! There's other busi-   315
    ness for thee.
Come, thou tortoise! When?

Enter ARIEL *like a water nymph.*
Fine apparition! My quaint Ariel,
Hark in thine ear.

Ariel   My lord, it shall be done. *Exit.*

Prospero Thou poisonous slave, got by the devil
    himself
Upon thy wicked dam, come forth!   320

Enter CALIBAN.

Caliban As wicked dew as e'er my mother brushed
With raven's feather from unwholesome fen
Drop on you both! A south-west blow on ye
And blister you all o'er!

Prospero For this, be sure, tonight thou shalt   325
    have cramps,
Side-stitches that shall pen thy breath up; urchins
Shall, for that vast of night that they may work,
All exercise on thee; thou shalt be pinched
As thick as honeycomb, each pinch more stinging
Than bees that made 'em.   330

Caliban   I must eat my dinner.
This island's mine by Sycorax my mother,
Which thou tak'st from me. When thou cam'st first,
Thou strok'st me and made much of me; wouldst
    give me
Water with berries in't; and teach me how
To name the bigger light, and how the less,   335
That burn by day and night; and then I loved thee
And showed thee all the qualities o' th' isle,
The fresh springs, brine-pits, barren place and
    fertile.

---

316.   *When?:* i.e., when are you coming? An expression of impatience.

317.   *quaint:* the word has various Early Modern meanings: skillful, ingenious, delicate, elegant.

323.   *A south-west:* this wind, because it carried warm, damp weather, was considered unhealthy.

326.   *pen:* the word combines the meanings of "to pen up" (enclose tightly) and "to pin" (jab painfully).

    urchins: hedgehogs, or malicious spirits who assumed their shape.

327.   *vast:* void or waste.

328.   *All exercise:* all work their tortures on you.

331.   *This . . . mother:* According to Caliban, Prospero is the usurper and Caliban the rightful master, by inheritance, of the island.

335.   *the bigger light:* the sun.

    the less: the moon.

337.   *qualities:* the resources.

Cursed be I that did so! All the charms
Of Sycorax — toads, beetles, bats, light on you!   340
For I am all the subjects that you have,
Which first was mine own king; and here you sty me
In this hard rock, whiles you do keep from me
The rest o' th' island.

Prospero   Thou most lying slave,
Whom stripes may move, not kindness! I have used   345
    thee
(Filth as thou art) with humane care, and lodged
    thee
In mine own cell till thou didst seek to violate
The honor of my child.

Caliban O ho, O ho! Would't had been done!
Thou didst prevent me; I had peopled else   350
This isle with Calibans.

Miranda   Abhorred slave,
Which any print of goodness wilt not take,
Being capable of all ill! I pitied thee,
Took pains to make thee speak, taught thee each
    hour
One thing or other: when thou didst not, savage,   355
Know thine own meaning, but wouldst gabble like
A thing most brutish, I endowed thy purposes
With words that made them known. But thy vile
    race,
Though thou didst learn, had that in't which good
    natures
Could not abide to be with; therefore wast thou   360
Deservedly confined into this rock, who hadst
Deserved more than a prison.

Caliban You taught me language, and my profit
    on't
Is, I know how to curse. The red plague rid you
For learning me your language!   365

Prospero   Hag-seed, hence!
Fetch us in fuel; and be quick, thou'rt best,
To answer other business. Shrug'st thou, malice

342.   *sty:* imprison, as in a pigsty.

345.   *stripes:* lashes of a whip.

351.   *Abhorred slave . . . :* Miranda's lines here reveal her anger over Caliban's attempted rape. She curses more effectively than he does (see below, line 364).

352.   *print of goodness:* education in virtue has no effect on Caliban.

358.   *race:* inherited nature.

359.   *good natures:* natural virtues.

364.   *red plague:* bubonic plague.

       rid: destroy. Note the compact, angry power in the near rhyme of "red" and "rid."

366.   *thou'rt best:* it were best for you.

367.   *malice:* Caliban is addressed as malice, or ill will, personified.

If thou neglect'st or dost unwillingly
What I command, I'll rack thee with old cramps,
Fill all thy bones with aches, make thee roar   370
That beasts shall tremble at thy din.

Caliban   No, pray thee.
[*Aside*] I must obey. His art is of such pow'r
It would control my dam's god, Setebos,
And make a vassal of him.

Prospero   So, slave; hence!

Exit CALIBAN.

Enter FERDINAND *and* ARIEL (*invisible*), *playing and
    singing.*

Ariel's song.
Come unto these yellow sands,   375
      And then take hands.
Curtsied when you have and kissed,
      The wild waves whist,
Foot it featly here and there;
And, sweet sprites, the burden bear   380
      Hark, hark!
      (*Burden, dispersedly:* Bowgh, wawgh!)
The watchdogs bark.
      (*Burden, dispersedly:* Bowgh, wawgh!)
Hark, hark! I hear   385
The strain of strutting Chanticleer
      Cry cock-a-diddle-dowe.

Ferdinand Where should this music be? I' th' air
      or th' earth?
It sounds no more; and sure it waits upon
Some god o' th' island. Sitting on a bank,   390
Weeping again the King my father's wrack.
This music crept by me upon the waters,
Allaying both their fury and my passion
With its sweet air. Thence I have followed it,
Or it hath drawn me rather; but 'tis gone.   395
No, it begins again.

Ariel's song.
Full fathom five thy father lies;

---

369. *old cramps:* the cramps that afflict the old.

371. *din:* roaring.

373. *dam's:* mother's.

Setebos: a god of the Patagonians; Shakespeare may have come across the name in an account of Magellan's voyages.

374. *vassal:* servant.

SD. *Ariel invisible:* Renaissance theatrical costumes included "a gown for to go invisible," which Ariel would wear here; the Japanese theater still uses special costumes to signal a character's invisibility.

378. *whist:* being stilled.

379. *featly:* nimbly.

380. *sweet . . . burden:* A chorus of sprites assists Ariel and sings in refrain. See above, line 193: "Ariel and all his quality."

SD. *Burden, dispersedly:* Chorus, from various locations, possibly including offstage.

386. *Chanticleer:* the traditional name of the rooster.

393. *Allaying:* i.e., calming both the raging sea and my grief with this sweet music.

397. *Full fathom five:* five fathoms = 30 feet.

Of his bones are coral made;
　Those are pearls that were his eyes;
　　Nothing of him that doth fade　　　　　　　　　　400
But doth suffer a sea-change
Into something rich and strange.
Sea nymphs hourly ring his knell:
　　(*Burden:* Dong-dong)
Hark! now I hear them — Ding-dong bell.　　　　　405

Ferdinand The ditty does remember my drowned
　father.
This is no mortal business, nor no sound
That the earth owes. I hear it now above me.

Prospero The fringed curtains of thine eye advance
And say what thou seest yond.　　　　　　　　　　410

Miranda　　　　　　　　　　What is't? a spirit?
Lord, how it looks about! Believe me, sir,
It carries a brave form. But 'tis a spirit.

Prospero No, wench: it eats, and sleeps, and hath
　such senses
As we have, such. This gallant which thou seest
Was in the wrack; and, but he's something stained　415
With grief (that's beauty's canker), thou mightst
　call him
A goodly person. He hath lost his fellows
And strays about to find 'em.

Miranda　　　　　　　　　I might call him
A thing divine; for nothing natural
I ever saw so noble.　　　　　　　　　　　　　　420

Prospero [*Aside*]　　It goes on, I see,
As my soul prompts it. Spirit, fine spirit, I'll free
　thee
Within two days for this.

Ferdinand　　　　　　　　Most sure, the goddess
On whom these airs attend! Vouchsafe my prayer
May know if you remain upon this island,
And that you will some good instruction give　　425
How I may bear me here. My prime request,

400.	*Nothing of him . . . But:* i.e., all of him that decays is also transformed into treasure.
406.	*does remember:* commemorates.
408.	*owes:* owns, produces.
409.	*fringed curtains . . . advance:* i.e., raise your eyelids. Prospero's language is deliberately elaborate and formal, like a magical spell or incantation.
412.	*brave:* handsome, attractive.
415.	*but:* except that.
	stained: disfigured.
418.	*strays:* wanders.
419.	*natural:* from the world of Nature, as opposed to the world of Spirit.
420.	*It goes on:* i.e., the plan works as I had intended.
422.	*Most sure:* certainly this must be.
423.	*these airs:* the music Ferdinand has been following.
424.	*remain upon:* inhabit.

Which I do last pronounce, is (O you wonder!)
If you be maid or no?

Miranda　　　　　　　　No wonder, sir,
But certainly a maid.

Ferdinand　　　　　　My language? Heavens!
I am the best of them that speak this speech,　　　430
Were I but where 'tis spoken.

Prospero　　　　　　　　How? the best?
What wert thou if the King of Naples heard thee?

Ferdinand A single thing, as I am now, that
　　　wonders
To hear thee speak of Naples. He does hear me;
And that he does I weep. Myself am Naples,　　　435
Who with mine eyes, never since at ebb, beheld
The King my father wracked.

Miranda　　　　　　　　Alack, for mercy!

Ferdinand Yes faith and all his lords the Duke
　　　of Milan
And his brave son being twain.

Prospero [*Aside*]　　　　　The Duke of Milan
And his more braver daughter could control thee,　　　440
If now 'twere fit to do't. At the first sight
They have changed eyes. Delicate Ariel,
I'll set thee free for this. — A word, good sir.
I fear you have done yourself some wrong. A word!

Miranda Why speaks my father so ungently? This　　　445
Is the third man that e'er I saw; the first
That e'er I sighed for. Pity move my father
To be inclined my way!

Ferdinand　　　　　　O, if a virgin
And your affection not gone forth, I'll make you
The Queen of Naples.　　　450

Prospero　　　　　Soft sir! one word more.
[*Aside*] They are both in either's pow'rs. But this
　　　swift business
I must uneasy make, lest too light winning

---

427. *O you wonder!:* a play on Miranda's name (from the Latin, *mirus*, meaning "wonderful") although Ferdinand does not yet know it.

433. *single:* (1) lonely, (2) weak.

434. *Naples:* King of Naples.

439. *son:* either Antonio's son (not elsewhere mentioned) or else "his" refers back to "Naples."

440. *control:* oppose or contradict.

442. *changed eyes:* fallen in love; exchanged looks of love.

444. *I fear . . . wrong:* polite irony for "you are mistaken."

449. *gone forth:* promised to someone already.

452–53. *light:* wordplay on multiple meanings; in the first line the word means, "easy"; in the next, "undervalued."

Make the prize light. — One word more! I charge
   thee
That thou attend me. Thou dost here usurp
The name thou ow'st not, and hast put thyself   455
Upon this island as a spy to win it
From me, the lord on't.

Ferdinand   No as I am a man!

Miranda There's nothing ill can dwell in such a
      temple.
If the ill spirit have so fair a house,
Good things will strive to dwell with't.   460

Prospero   Follow me. —
Speak not you for him; he's a traitor. — Come!
I'll manacle thy neck and feet together;
Sea water shalt thou drink; thy food shall be
The fresh-brook mussels withered roots and husks
Wherein the acorn cradled. Follow!   465

Ferdinand   No.
I will resist such entertainment till
Mine enemy has more power.

He draws, and is charmed from moving

Miranda   O dear father,
Make not too rash a trial of him, for
He's gentle, and not fearful.

Prospero   What, I say,
My foot my tutor? — Put thy sword up, traitor!   470
Who mak'st a show but dar'st not strike, thy
      conscience
Is so possessed with guilt. Come, from thy ward!
For I can here disarm thee with this stick
And make thy weapon drop.

Miranda   Beseech you, father!

Prospero Hence! Hang not on my garments.   475

Miranda Sir, have pity.
I'll be his surety.

455.	*ow'st:* ownest.
458.	*in such a temple:* a conventional Renaissance idea, ultimately derived from Plato, that the body reflects the soul's virtue.
464 ff.	Prospero here describes a coarse diet as part of his plan to deprive and test Ferdinand's professed love for Miranda.
SD.	*charmed from moving:* by a gesture from Prospero.
488.	*trial:* judgment.
469.	*gentle:* a gentleman.
	fearful: either (1) cowardly, or (2) to be feared.
470.	*My foot my tutor?:* i.e., am I to be instructed by something beneath me?
472.	*ward:* the defensive stance assumed by a fencer.
476.	*surety:* guarantee.

Prospero   Silence! One word more
Shall make me chide thee, if not hate thee. What,
An advocate for an impostor? Hush!
Thou think'st there is no more such shapes as he,
Having seen but him and Caliban. Foolish wench!   480
To th' most of men this is a Caliban,
And they to him are angels.

Miranda   My affections
Are then most humble. I have no ambition
To see a goodlier man.

Prospero   Come on, obey!
Thy nerves are in their infancy again   485
And have no vigor in them.

Ferdinand   So they are.
My spirits, as in a dream, are all bound up.
My father's loss, the weakness which I feel,
The wrack of all my friends, nor this man's threats
To whom I am subdued, are but light to me,   490
Might I but through my prison once a day
Behold this maid. All corners else o' th' earth
Let liberty make use of. Space enough
Have I in such a prison.

Prospero [*Aside*]   It works.
[*To* FERDINAND] Come on. —   495
[*To* ARIEL] Thou hast done well, fine Ariel!
[*To* FERDINAND] Follow me.
[*To* ARIEL] Hark what thou else shalt do me.

Miranda   Be of comfort
My father's of a better nature, sir,
Than he appears by speech. This is unwonted
Which now came from him.

Prospero   Thou shalt be as free
As mountain winds; but then exactly do   500
All points of my command.

Ariel   To th' syllable.

Prospero Come, follow. — Speak not for him. *Exeunt*

481.   *to:* compared to.

482.   *affections:* requirements of love.

485.   *nerves:* sinews or muscular strength.

493.   *Let liberty . . . of:* i.e., let those who are free make use of all the corners of the world; I am happy in any place where I can look on Miranda.

500.   *but then:* but until then.

502.   *Speak not . . . :* addressed to Miranda, telling her, again, not to intercede on Ferdinand's behalf.

COMMENTARY

Shakespeare uses this long *expository scene* (a scene that exposes facts) to introduce the majority of the play's central characters and to provide the background information necessary for understanding how Prospero and his daughter Miranda came to live on the island.

In this regard, the scene follows the traditional five-act structure of plays, an inheritance of Classical Greek and Roman drama and the theories of effective drama outlined by Aristotle in his *Poetics*. The opening action of the play, which introduces characters and situation, is known as the *protasis* or *exposition*.

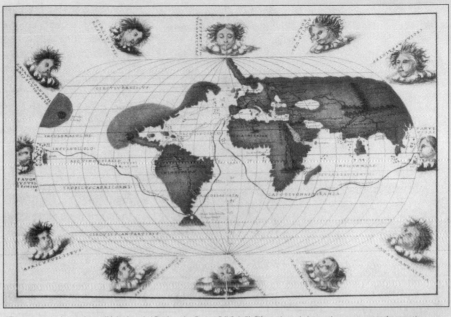

"The sea, mounting to the welkin's cheek / Dashes the fire out" (I.2.4–5). Fifteenth- and sixteenth-century maps frequently showed the winds as faced with puffed cheeks, blowing on the waters. Miranda refers to this, combining it with the idea of the face of heaven blowing against the tempestuous sea in her description of "the welkin's cheek."
The Huntington Library, Art Collections, and Botanical Gardens, San Marino, California/SuperStock

The shape of *The Tempest* as a play is also informed by a popular tradition of entertainment for King James and his court, known as *masques*. Masques were elaborate, ballet-like productions of song and dance in which the noble gentlemen and ladies of the court danced the principal roles. This form of entertainment follows a basic pattern in which an *anti-masque*, a scene of *cacophony* (a jumble of unpleasant noises) and disorder, is replaced by musical harmony and order in the masque proper. This change is brought about by a noble or divine agent, who frequently is meant to represent the King. Keep this in mind as you observe the extent to which Prospero exercises his authority to reestablish order from chaos.

The principal function of this scene is to introduce the characters and the background events of betrayal that have set the present story into action. By its very nature, this scene runs the risk of being dull, because it is so rich in information. Shakespeare is too skilled of a writer to fall into this trap, however. The audience is immediately struck by his ability to quickly and compactly establish the nature of his characters and the history of events leading up to the shipwreck scene, which the audience has just witnessed.

Miranda, too, witnesses this scene, and her initial lines reveal immediately her sensitivity and concern. She feels great empathy with the sailors on board the tempest-tossed ship proclaiming, "I have suffered / With those that I saw suffer" (lines 5–6).

Prospero calms Miranda, just as he has calmed the stormy seas, and assures her that all of the ship's passengers are alive and unharmed. He then calls on Miranda to help him take off his magic garment — probably a large cloak — which, along with a book and staff, make up the props that present Prospero as a *magus*, or scholarly magician.

Prospero is also a father and reveals in the discussion with Miranda that follows that he is generally a kind and concerned one but is nonetheless strict. He alone has cared for and raised Miranda for the past twelve years, serving as her father, mother, protector, and schoolmaster. We get a glimpse in this scene of what his instruction as a schoolmaster must be like, as he delivers a lengthy history lecture — one that clearly moves him (note the jumbled nature of some of his sentences

"Lie there my Art" (I.2.25). Prospero is a magus or scholarly magician and, in these lines, refers to the cloak or magic garment he wears while practicing his magical arts. Palazzo della Ragione, Padua, Italy/SuperStock

and the frequent *elisions* or contraction of words suggesting that his passions nearly burst beyond his words). He stops occasionally to make sure his pupil remains attentive and understands the lesson. Miranda's replies indicate that she does indeed listen closely. Her sensitive nature causes her to be strongly moved by her father's tale.

The tale is quite a fantastic one: Miranda is a princess, Prospero reveals, and he was formerly the Duke of Milan. As a leader, Prospero lost interest in taking care of the day-to-day business of government; he became far more interested in his studies. Prospero placed the duty of managing his Dukedom in his brother Antonio's hands. But Antonio grew greedy and staged a rebellion against Prospero with the aid of Alonso, King of Naples. Gathering an army with Alonso's help, Antonio took over Milan and had Prospero and the infant Miranda thrust into a leaky boat and put out to sea. Gonzalo, a loyal friend to Prospero, took care to provide the two exiles with food and fresh water, along with some of the prized volumes from Prospero's library. Now, twelve years later, events

have allowed for Prospero to use his magic — especially his control over the weather — to bring those who betrayed him to the same island on which he and his daughter were cast away some dozen years before.

Prospero's story provides a vehicle for the audience to learn more about both his character and Miranda's and also provides more background and character information on the court party briefly introduced in the previous scene. Antonio is cast in the role of principal villain and the possible character on whom Prospero particularly desires revenge. Has Prospero brought Antonio and Alonso safely through the storm only to torment and punish them, to show them the darkness of their crimes before killing them?

As Prospero's evil brother Antonio says, "what's past is prologue": Prospero and Miranda's story is background to the present scene and, after Prospero finishes telling it (line 184), the action of the play begins to move forward — but not before a magical pause in which time effectively stands still. Prospero charms Miranda into a sleep so that he can communicate with Ariel, the airy spirit who performs Prospero's magical business.

It is clear that Prospero is a practitioner of white magic and not *necromancy,* or black magic. His magical works involve controlling the weather and causing friendly spirits to appear in order to perform helpful work or shows. He does not summon devils or deal in torture, although he does threaten Ariel with imprisonment in the knotty entrails of an oak tree and, according to Caliban, is prone to subjecting Caliban with cramps and other torments when the earthy slave is less than willing to do his chores.

Prospero asks Ariel the time and learns that it is "two glasses" past "the midseason" — two hours, in other words, past noon. This was the traditional starting time for plays in the public theatres, which had to capitalize on daylight for performance. Prospero and Ariel further remark that the remainder of their work must take place between now and six. Shakespeare is closely following the precept suggested by Aristotle (and religiously followed by Shakespeare's contemporary and frequent critic, Ben Jonson) to obey the unity of time. This meant that the action of the play would not span more than a twenty-four hour period. Shakespeare goes one better here, making the actual playing time of the play and the story itself very nearly coincide. The playing time was likely close to the frequently referenced two hours' traffic of the stage, whereas the elapsed time of the story itself, as revealed here, is about four hours in duration.

The opening shipwreck scene is recalled in the conversation between Prospero and Ariel. Ariel has followed Prospero's commands precisely and is anxious to be rewarded with long-promised freedom. When Ariel raises the question of being set free, however, Prospero is enraged. He reminds Ariel of the imprisonment inside a pine tree from which Prospero set Ariel free upon arriving on the island, and of Ariel's former servitude to the witch Sycorax. Ariel is in Prospero's debt. This is a traditional relationship between magician and spirit; there is invariably a sort of contract in which the magical spirit is bound to serve (note, for example, the famous story of Aladdin and the genie where the genie is under obligation, after being set free from the lamp, to grant whomever frees the genie three wishes). It is never a wholly equal or willing partnership. This explains the tension surrounding Ariel's demand for freedom and

Prospero's angry reaction. Prospero threatens Ariel with twelve years of imprisonment in an oak tree. Since Ariel is a spirit as free as the wind, one can easily understand Ariel's dislike of confinement.

Ariel's self-description of flaming amazement and burning distinctly in various parts of the ship suggests that Ariel appeared to the sailors as the meteorological phenomenon known as St. Elmo's Fire. This bluish-white, flame-like apparition is actually caused by atmospheric electricity. It was long held as an omen for sailors. Sir Francis Bacon, a near-contemporary of Shakespeare and a pioneering scientist, wrote about this phenomenon, drawing on the writings of the Roman naturalist Pliny, stating, "If it [St. Elmo's Fire] be single, [it] prognosticates a severe storm, which will be much more severe if the ball [of flame] does not adhere to the mast, but rolls or dances about. But if there are two of them, and that too, when the storm has increased, it is reckoned a good sign. But if there are three of them, the storm will become more fearful" (from "History of the Winds" in *The Works of Francis Bacon,* ed. James Spedding, et al. Vol 9: 453. Cambridge: Riverside Press, 1869). Notice that Ariel claims to have burned distinctly in three places: the topmast, the yards, and the boresprit, thus throwing the superstitious sailors into considerable terror. They are deliberately led to

"Now he was / The ivy which hid my princely trunk" (I.2.85–86). Prospero's imagery in these lines presents himself as a tree and his brother, Antonio, as the parasitic ivy that feeds off the healthy tree rather than producing for itself.

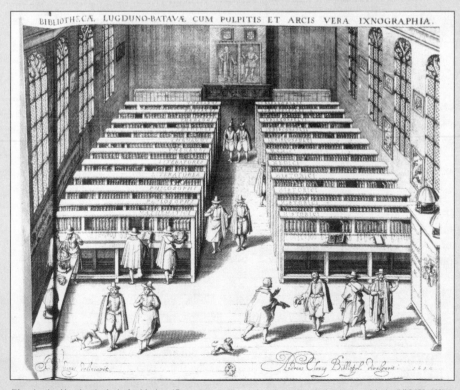

"Knowing that I loved my books, he furnished me / From mine own library with volumes that / I prize above my dukedom" (I.2.166–168). Prospero's learning is symbolized by his books, his magic garment, and his magical staff. It was as a result of Prospero being too involved in his studies that he was removed from his post as Duke of Milan, but it is also through learning that he will regain his political power.

Explorer/SuperStock

believe that the storm is about to get worse, thus increasing their fears and strengthening their beliefs that they are about to drown.

Through Prospero and Ariel's conversation, still more of the history of Prospero and Miranda's arrival on the island is revealed. We learn that the island had another inhabitant, in addition to Ariel, when Prospero first arrived, Caliban, who is variously described as a "moon-calf" or "monster," "demi-devil," and "a freckled whelp, hag born."

Ariel and Caliban balance one another as the embodiments of air (or spirit) and earth. Ariel's name is suggestive of both air and that of an archangel. The significance of Caliban's name has been the subject of a good deal of scholarly debate. The two principal lines of argument are that in "Caliban" Shakespeare has set up an anagram for "canibal." This might also, then, be a reference to Canibalism as part of the New World setting. Ariel speaks of the "still-vexed" or stormy "Bermoothes" (line 229), possibly hinting at the location of Prospero's island (although the name also refers to a disreputable part of sixteenth-century London). We find out later that the Italian noblemen — Alonso, Antonio, Sebastian, and Gonzalo — and their attendants were travelling on their return journey to Italy from the wedding of Alonso's daughter, Claribel, in Tunis in North Africa. The second suggestion concerning the origin of Caliban's name is that Shakespeare took it from a gypsy word, "cauliban" or "kaliban," meaning "black." Both explanations for the possible source of Caliban's name coincide with Caliban's earthy character, which is a deliberate contrast to Ariel's airy and delicate nature.

Caliban's animalistic tendencies are further revealed in the fact that he previously sought to rape Miranda, or, as Prospero genteelly puts it, "didst seek to violate / The honor of my child"(lines

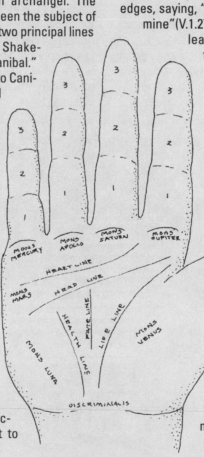

"Transported / And rapt in secret studies" (I.2.76–77). Prospero has studied "white magic," which allows him to better understand the mysteries of the weather and perhaps also of the human body. He does not practice black magic or necromancy, which involves the summoning of devils and demons.

349–350). Caliban regrets that he was prevented from doing so and, thus, had his plot to have "peopled else / This isle with Calibans"(lines 352–353) foiled by Prospero. Caliban is not done hatching plans of rebellion, as we will soon see.

The relationship between Prospero, Miranda, Ariel, and Caliban should be read in part as that of a family. As noted in the Introduction, the patriarchal structure of the Early Modern family extended the father figure's authority to his servants as well as his children. Among Prospero's three "children." Miranda is clearly Prospero's favorite, with Ariel in the second position; Caliban (who at the play's end Prospero grudgingly acknowledges, saying, "this thing of darkness I / Acknowledge mine"(V.1.275–276)) clearly takes up the position of least-favored child. One need only look to the terms with which Prospero addresses each of his "children" to get a sense of their pecking order. Miranda is his "dear one," "a cherubin," and he frequently acknowledges her as "dear" and "my daughter." Ariel is similarly possessed in a loving manner, being frequently referred to as "my delicate Ariel," and "my Ariel chick," among other forms. Prospero frequently praises Ariel for industry and cleverness. Caliban, on the other hand, is subject to a much coarser, more distant set of names and is never the subject of compliments from Prospero. Here, when first introduced, he is called forth as a "slave;" he is also referred to as "earth," "hagseed," a "tortoise," and "filth," among other less than complimentary terms.

Similarly, the words Caliban and Ariel say distinguishes them. Ariel speaks initially of fire and amazement, of spiritual elements and, specifically, the higher elements that comprise the universe in an Early Modern understanding (see the

Introduction on the elements and humors). Caliban represents and speaks of the lower, earthy elements, of water and earth, referring specifically to "springs, brine-pits, barren place and fertile." Ariel rides on the "curled clouds" and runs upon "the sharp wind of the North," while Caliban's principal duty is to fetch in firewood when not caged in "this hard rock." The distinctions between these two characters is not that easily black and white, however. Ariel is not perfect and his fiery nature is displayed in this scene as moodiness and a jealous desire for freedom. Caliban, similarly, is not as thoroughly dull and coarse as Prospero makes him out to be. In later praise of the beauty of the island and of Miranda, Caliban speaks some of the play's most lyrical lines.

Ariel's reference to the "still-vexed" or stormy "Bermoothes" (I.2.229) has led many readers of the play to believe that the play is set in Bermuda and thus intended to be a presentation of the New World, possibly even America. The final years of Elizabeth I's reign (she died in 1603 and was succeed by James VI of Scotland, who thus became James I of England) and the early years of James I's reign saw the massive growth of colonial enterprise by England and other European nations in the Americas. Other details in the play — such as the fact that Alonso and company are traveling from Tunis, in North Africa, back to Italy suggests that the likelihood of the play taking place in some sort of American or truly New World setting is impractical and unlikely. Indeed, if one were to locate a precise island that Shakespeare had in mind when writing the play, it seems more plausible that it would be located somewhere in the Mediterranean rather than out in the middle of the Atlantic.

Ultimately, what is important is that the play takes place on an island, a limited and isolated land mass where Prospero is fully and completely the master of his domain. Furthermore, it is a place of magic and imagination, a place slightly separated from the everyday and the familiar, and thus very like the playhouse in which the play itself is being presented.

Many readers see the relationship between Prospero and Ariel and Caliban — and especially Prospero's treatment of Caliban — as commentary on European colonialism of the New World. Caliban is brutish and brutally treated. As he is introduced to the audience by Prospero and Miranda, a composite picture of despicableness emerges. We learn that this was not necessarily always so. Caliban claims that Prospero was at first kind, and

that in exchange for this kindness, Caliban shared the beauties and natural riches of the island freely with Prospero and his child. Prospero and Miranda taught Caliban to speak but were eventually betrayed by Caliban's desire to rape Miranda. As Prospero says, Caliban is more moved by *stripes* (by beating) than by kindness, and is a creature "on whose nature / Nurture can never stick." Just as scholars are today, Early Modern thinkers were greatly interested in issues of human behavior and debated whether behavior was the product of nature (the traits with which we are born) or nurture (social conditioning and environment). The statement that emerges with Caliban is that an essentially primitive or animalistic creature can be elevated to a degree, but his savagery can never be wholly erased.

In the *Dramatis personae*, or list of characters, for *The Tempest* as first published in 1623, Caliban is referred to as a "salvage and deformed slave" (this edition has modernized the term to the more familiar form, "savage"). Many writers in Shakespeare's day were fascinated with the savages they encountered when traveling on explorations to the New World. One of these writers, the French essayist Michele de Montaigne, wrote a particularly famous essay entitled "Of the Cannibals." This essay, along with several others, was translated into English in 1603 by John Florio and was clearly read by Shakespeare (as is more fully detailed in the discussion of Act II, Scene 1). In this essay, Montaigne argues that the savage cannibals have an inherent goodness and that they obey certain universal elements of natural law, even if they clearly know nothing of European manners and man-made laws. Montaigne, ultimately, sees considerable good and potential in the savages he encountered. Other Early Modern travelers were less optimistic about the foreign peoples they met. The extent to which Caliban is viewed as

"Some time I'd divide, / And burn in many places; on the topmast, / The yards and boresprit, would I flame distinctly (I.2.198–200). Ariel takes the form of lightning-like fire when appearing to the sailors in the midst of the opening tempest. Ariel specifically mentions appearing in three distinct places: the topmast, the yards (horizontal beams attached to the mast and from which the sails hang), and the boresprit or bowsprit (the spar of lumber at the prow of the ship, illustrated here).

irredeemably evil or more victimized than victimizer is ultimately up to the audience and is an element that can be manipulated for a specific interpretation in performance.

Just as Ariel and Caliban are held up for comparison to one another by Ariel exiting at line 318 and Caliban being called forth to attend to Prospero in the same line, so is Caliban's exit at line 375 dove-tailed with Ariel's reentry with an as yet unmet character, Alonso's son, Ferdinand. Ariel guides Ferdinand with song, two lyrical ballads that praise the beauty of the island and the mystery of death, or, more accurately (because Alonso and the court party are only supposed drowned by Ferdinand), feigned death. The lyrical and heartfelt grief Ferdinand expresses is perhaps the first clue that the direction of this play may well prove that of a romantic comedy rather than a revenge tragedy. Miranda has been awakened for the interaction with Caliban, and in her angry reaction to him and the memory of his attempted rape of her, we witness another aspect of Miranda's character. She has her father's temper and sense of righteous indignation towards those who betray her. Some editors in the past have assigned the lines from 351 and following ("Abhorred slave . . .") to Prospero. Doing so robs Miranda's character of some of the complexity with which Shakespeare saw her. Although a young woman, and one who has grown up in a sheltered environment, she is nonetheless well educated, thanks to her father. In addition to actual lessons learned at his instruction, Miranda has learned and internalized a great deal simply by observing and growing to be like her father.

Ferdinand is immediately far more attractive physically and verbally than Caliban, and the juxtaposing of their introductions to the audience is meant to convey this. Prospero has separated Ferdinand from the remainder of the court party for a deliberate purpose. Although part of that reason may yet prove an aid to exacting murderous revenge on Antonio and Alonso, the initial reason for it is to introduce Ferdinand to Miranda. Prospero's commentary as the young lovers meet and fall directly into love at first sight reveals that their mutual attraction was indeed an important part of his design. Ferdinand and Miranda pay one another similar and equally exalted compliments by believing the other to be a spirit or god.

Ferdinand offers marriage within only minutes of first glimpsing Miranda, so moved is he by Miranda's beauty and purity. As he observes, he is no stranger to feminine beauty and charm but nonetheless sees Miranda, as Caliban will later term her, "a non pareil," one without equal. Miranda is similarly smitten with Ferdinand; they have, as Prospero notes "changed eyes." But the course of true love must know at least some challenge if it is to withstand the test of time. Prospero must put some challenges before Ferdinand to make certain that his love is true, and to make him earn the right to marry Miranda. If simply handed the prize without work, he will not value it: "But this swift business / I must uneasy make lest too light winning / Make the prize light" (lines 451–453).

Prospero decides upon a course that will test the resolve of both of the young lovers. We see him near the end of the scene playing a part, specifically the role of a guarded and overly protective, almost tyrannical father. He plays the part to perfection, threatening Ferdinand with harsh treatment and a coarse diet and warning Miranda that if she displeases or disobeys him, he will withhold his love. All the while, he is thrilled by the immediate bond Ferdinand and Miranda feel, and praises Ariel for helping him with this matchmaking.

Ferdinand is not alone in undergoing a test at Prospero's hands. Every character in the play is similarly tested and judged by Prospero. In this regard, it is necessary to remember the play's original audience. Although it is believed that the play was performed at the Blackfriars Theatre and possibly also at the Globe, the first two (and only recorded) performances of this play were at the Banqueting House at Whitehall. In this setting, the principal member of the audience was King James I himself, a King who had written a book on *Daemonologie* — magical arts including witchcraft, sorcery, and demonic arts — and considered himself as the father and great teacher of all his subjects. Prospero, the father figure and great teacher of this play, is clearly meant as a representation of James.

Notes

Notes

THE TEMPEST
ACT II

Sebastian *You were kneeled to and importuned otherwise*
    By all of us; and the fair soul herself
    Weighed between loathness and obedience, at
    Which end o' th' beam should bow. We have lost your son,
    I fear, for ever. Milan and Naples have
    Moe widows in them of this business' making
    Than we bring men to comfort them:
    The fault's your own.

Act II, Scene 1

Elsewhere on the island, the King and his attendants search for Ferdinand. Their attitudes toward the search and the likelihood of finding the prince alive reveals a great deal about their characters: Alonso sadly despairs that the prince is lost forever; Gonzalo is optimistic; Sebastian and Antonio are sarcastic and reveal to one another privately that they hope Ferdinand is drowned. A strange sleep overcomes all but Sebastian and Antonio, who intend to take advantage of this strange opportunity by murdering Alonso and Gonzalo. Ariel arrives in time to awaken Gonzalo and Antonio and prevent the double-murder.

ACT II, SCENE 1
[Another part of the island.]

Enter ALONSO, SEBASTIAN, ANTONIO, GONZALO, ADRIAN, FRANCISCO, *and Others.*

Gonzalo Beseech you, sir, be merry. You have cause
  (So have we all) of joy; for our escape
  Is much beyond our loss. Our hint of woe
  Is common: every day some sailor's wife,
  The masters of some merchant, and the merchant,   5
  Have just our theme of woe; but for the miracle,
  I mean our preservation, few in millions
  Can speak like us. Then wisely, good sir, weigh
  Our sorrow with our comfort.

Alonso   Prithee peace.

Sebastian He receives comfort like cold porridge.   10

Antonio The visitor will not give him o'er so.

Sebastian Look, he's winding up the watch of his
  wit; by and by it will strike.

Gonzalo Sir —

Sebastian One. Tell.   15

Gonzalo When every grief is entertained, that's
    offered
  Comes to th' entertainer —

Sebastian A dollar.

Gonzalo Dolor comes to him, indeed. You have
  spoken truer than you purposed.   20

NOTES

3. *hint:* occasion.

5. *The master . . . the merchant:* i.e., the master of a merchant or commercial ship, and the merchant who owns the ship.

10. *He:* Alonso.

  porridge: with a pun on Alonso's "peace" and pease-porridge (as in the nursery rhyme, "pease-porridge hot. . . .").

11. *The visitor:* the allusion is to the church official, known as the visitor, who gave comfort to the sick.

  give him o'er: leave him alone.

13. *strike:* the reference is to the repeating or striking watch of the sixteenth century.

15. *One. Tell:* i.e., he has struck one; keep count.

16. *that's:* which is.

17–19. *th' entertainer . . . dollar . . . Dolor:* i.e., when an entertainer helps his audience to laugh away their sadness he is paid that which he was offered: a dollar as payment. Gonzalo puns on this with "Dolor," meaning "grief"; the entertainer takes grief away as one would haul off old junk.

Sebastian You have taken it wiselier than I meant
you should.

Gonzalo Therefore, my lord —

Antonio Fie, what a spendthrift is he of his tongue!

Alonso I prithee spare.   25

Gonzalo Well, I have done. But yet —

Sebastian He will be talking.

Antonio Which, of he or Adrian, for a good wager,
first begins to crow?

Sebastian The old cock.   30

Antonio The cock'rel.

Sebastian Done! The wager?

Antonio A laughter.

Sebastian A match!

Adrian Though this island seem to be desert —   35

Antonio Ha, ha, ha!

Sebastian So, you're paid.

Adrian Uninhabitable and almost inaccessible —

Sebastian Yet —

Adrian Yet —   40

Antonio He could not miss't.

Adrian It must needs be of subtle, tender, and
delicate temperance.

Antonio Temperance was a delicate wench.

Sebastian Ay, and a subtle, as he most learnedly   45
delivered.

Adrian The air breathes upon us here most sweetly.

Sebastian As if it had lungs, and rotten ones.

Antonio Or as 'twere perfumed by a fen.

Gonzalo Here is everything advantageous to life.   50

Antonio True; save means to live.

25. *spare:* i.e., spare me what you are about to say.

30–31. *the old cock . . . the cock'rel:* Gonzalo . . . Adrian.

33. *a laughter:* i.e., the winner has the right to laugh.

43. *temperance:* climate.

44. *Temperance:* woman's proper name; a particularly popular name among Puritans.

45. *subtle:* crafty, sexually aware.

Sebastian Of that there's none, or little.

Gonzalo How lush and lusty the grass looks! how green!

Antonio The ground indeed is tawny.   55

Sebastian With an eye of green in't.

Antonio He misses not much.

Sebastian No; he doth but mistake the truth totally.

Gonzalo But the rarity of it is, — which is indeed   60
almost beyond credit, —

Sebastian As many vouched rarities are.

Gonzalo That our garments, being, as they were,
drenched in the sea, hold, notwithstanding, their
freshness and gloss, being rather new-dyed than   65
stained with salt water.

Antonio If but one of his pockets could speak,
would it not say he lies?

Sebastian Ay, or very falsely pocket up his report.

Gonzalo Methinks our garments are now as fresh   70
as when we put them on first in Afric, at the marriage of the King's fair daughter Claribel to the
King of Tunis.

Sebastian 'Twas a sweet marriage, and we prosper well in our return.   75

Adrian Tunis was never graced before with such
a paragon to their queen.

Gonzalo Not since widow Dido's time.

Antonio Widow? A pox o' that! How came that
"widow" in? Widow Dido!   80

Sebastian What if he had said "widower Aeneas"
too? Good Lord, how you take it!

Adrian "Widow Dido," said you? You make me
study of that. She was of Carthage, not of Tunis.

Gonzalo This Tunis, sir, was Carthage.   85

55. *tawny:* burned by the sun to a dry brown.

56. *eye:* center, or spot.

62. *vouched rarities:* wonders said to be true but hard to believe or "almost beyond credit."

67. *If but . . . lies:* i.e., if he examined himself (and his pockets) closely, he would see his mistake.

74–75. *and we prosper:* a continuation of the sour irony present in most of what Sebastian and Antonio say.

78. *widow Dido:* Dido, a familiar classical figure to the Elizabethans, was usually thought of as the lover of Aeneas, not the widow (as she was) of Sychaeus; presumably this unfashionable "mistake" is the cause of Antonio's sophisticated laughter. This is followed by Gonzalo's confusion of Tunis and Carthage (see Commentary). The point of the whole passage is to show Antonio and Sebastian making fun of Gonzalo. He makes mistakes and is a good man. They, on the other hand, are technically correct, morally corrupt.

Adrian Carthage?

Gonzalo I assure you, Carthage.

Antonio His word is more than the miraculous harp.

Sebastian He hath raised the wall and houses too.

Antonio What impossible matter will he make easy   90
next?

Sebastian I think he will carry this island home in
his pocket and give it his son for an apple.

Antonio And, sowing the kernels of it in the sea.
bring forth more islands.   95

Gonzalo Ay!

Antonio Why, in good time.

Gonzalo Sir, we were talking that our garments
seem now as fresh as when we were at Tunis at the
marriage of your daughter, who is now Queen.   100

Antonio And the rarest that e'er came there.

Sebastian Bate, I beseech you, widow Dido.

Antonio O, widow Dido? Ay, widow Dido.

Gonzalo Is not, sir, my doublet as fresh as the first
day I wore it? I mean, in a sort.   105

Antonio That "sort" was well fished for.

Gonzalo When I wore it at your daughter's
marriage.

Alonso You cram these words into mine ears
against
The stomach of my sense. Would I had never   110
Married my daughter there, for coming thence
My son is lost; and, in my rate, she too,
Who is so far from Italy removed
I ne'er again shall see her. O thou mine heir
Of Naples and of Milan, what strange fish   115
Hath made his meal on thee?

Francisco   Sir, he may live.
I saw him beat the surges under him
And ride upon their backs. He trod the water,

88.	*miraculous harp:* Amphion's harp, which raised the walls of Thebes.
96.	*Ay!:* Gonzalo has been pondering his assertion that Carthage and Tunis are the same city. He here convinces himself again.
102.	*Bate:* except for; meant sarcastically.
105.	*in a sort:* more or less, comparatively.
106.	*That . . . for:* i.e., you are wise to qualify in it that way; again, meant sarcastically.
109–110.	*You cram . . . sense:* You force these words into my ears, although my mind has no desire to hear them.
112.	*rate:* opinion.

Whose enmity he flung aside, and breasted
The surge most swol'n that met him. His bold head   120
'Bove the contentious waves he kept, and oared
Himself with his good arms in lusty stroke
To th' shore, that o'er his wave-worn basis bowed,
As stooping to relieve him. I not doubt
He came alive to land.   125

Alonso   No, no, he's gone.

Sebastian Sir, you may thank yourself for this
great loss,
That would not bless our Europe with your daughter,
But rather loose her to an African,
Where she, at least, is banished from your eye
Who hath cause to wet the grief on't.   130

Alonso   Prithee peace.

Sebastian You were kneeled to and importuned
otherwise
By all of us; and the fair soul herself
Weighed, between loathness and obedience, at
Which end o' th' beam should bow. We have lost
your son,
I fear, for ever. Milan and Naples have   135
Moe widows in them of this business' making
Than we bring men to comfort them:
The fault's your own.

Alonso   So is the dear'st o' th' loss.

Gonzalo My Lord Sebastian,
The truth you speak doth lack some gentleness,   140
And time to speak it in. You rub the sore
When you should bring the plaster.

Sebastian   Very well.

Antonio And most chirurgeonly.

Gonzalo It is foul weather in us all, good sir,
When you are cloudy.   145

Sebastian   Foul weather?

Antonio   Very foul.

Gonzalo Had I plantation of this isle, my lord —

123. *that o'er . . . him:* Francisco's description suggests that, as Ferdinand struggled to keep his head above the waves, it appeared as though the cliffs bent over to help him and bring him to dry land.

128. *loose her:* mate her with

129–130. *from your . . . on't:* i.e., from you, who have cause to weep for her.

133–134. *Weighed . . . bow:* i.e., Claribel was torn between two dislikes: marrying a man she didn't choose or disobeying her father.

136. *Moe:* more.

138. *dear'st:* most deeply felt.

141. *time:* the suitable time.

142. *plaster:* bandage

143. *chirurgeonly:* like a surgeon.

146. *plantation:* Gonzalo means the colonization of governorship, but Antonio and Sebastian choose to understand the literal sense of sowing seeds.

Antonio He'd sow't with nettle seed.

Sebastian   Or docks, or mallows,

Gonzalo And were the king on't, what would I do?

Sebastian Scape being drunk for want of wine.

Gonzalo I' th' commonwealth I would by contraries   150
Execute all things; for no kind of traffic
Would I admit; no name of magistrate;
Letters should not be known; riches, poverty,
And use of service, none; contract, succession,
Bourn, bound of land, tilth, vineyard, none;   155
No use of metal, corn, or wine, or oil;
No occupation; all men idle, all;
And women too, but innocent and pure;
No sovereignty.

Sebastian   Yet he would be king on't.

Antonio The latter end of his commonwealth for-   160
gets the beginning.

Gonzalo All things in common nature should
         produce
Without sweat or endeavor. Treason, felony,
Sword, pike, knife, gun, or need of any engine
Would I not have; but nature should bring forth,   165
Of it own kind, all foison, all abundance,
To feed my innocent people.

Sebastian No marrying 'mong his subjects?

Antonio None, man, all idle — whores and knaves.

Gonzalo I would with such perfection govern, sir,   170
T' excel the golden age.

Sebastian   Save his Majesty!

Antonio Long live Gonzalo!

Gonzalo   And — do you mark me, sir?

Alonso Prithee no more. Thou dost talk nothing
to me.

Gonzalo I do well believe your Highness; and did   175
it to minister occasion to these gentlemen, who are

149.   *Scape:* escape, avoid.

150.   *by contraries:* in contrast to the usual practice.

151.   *traffic:* trade, commerce.

153.   *Letters:* both written documents, particularly of ownership and literature, academic study.

154.   *use of service:* practice of having servants.

         succession: inheritance.

155.   *Bourn, bound:* boundaries of private property; the two words are synonyms.

         tilth: arable (farmable) land.

160.   *forgets:* i.e., Gonzalo says if he were king there would be no sovereign — a contradiciton in logic.

164.   *engine:* of war; i.e., cannon.

166.   *it:* its.

         foison: harvest, abundance.

173.   *nothing to me:* i.e., nothing that you say makes any sense to me.

176.   *minister occasion:* provide an opportunity.

of such sensible and nimble lungs that they always
use to laugh at nothing.

Antonio 'Twas you we laughed at.

Gonzalo Who in this kind of merry fooling am   180
nothing to you: so you may continue, and laugh at
nothing still.

Antonio What a blow was there given!

Sebastian An it had not fall'n flatlong.

Gonzalo You are gentlemen of brave mettle: you   185
would lift the moon out of her sphere if she would
continue in it five weeks without changing.

Enter ARIEL [*invisible*] *playing solemn music.*

Sebastian We would so, and then go a-batfowling.

Antonio Nay, good my lord, be not angry.

Gonzalo No, I warrant you: I will not adventure   190
my discretion so weakly. Will you laugh me asleep,
for I am very heavy?

Antonio Go sleep, and hear us.

[*All sleep except* ALONSO, SEBASTIAN, *and* ANTONIO.]

Alonso What, all so soon asleep? I wish mine eyes
Would, with themselves, shut up my thoughts. I find   195
They are inclined to do so.

Sebastian   Please you, sir,
Do not omit the heavy offer of it.
It seldom visits sorrow; when it doth,
It is a comforter.

Antonio   We two, my lord,
Will guard your person while you take your rest,   200
And watch your safety.

Alonso Thank you. Wondrous heavy.

[ALONSO *sleeps. Exit* ARIEL.]

Sebastian What a strange drowsiness possesses
them!

Antonio It is the quality o' th' climate.

---

177. *sensible and nimble:* sensitive and active.

184. *An:* if

      flatlong: with the flat of the sword and not the edge.

186. *lift the moon . . . :* i.e., you would take the moon out of its orbit if you could reach it.

188. *a-batfowling:* (with the moon for a lantern) they would hunt birds with clubs (bats) while the birds slept in the trees at night.

190. *adventure my discretion:* risk my reputation.

191. *so weakly:* in such an insignificant matter.

193. *Go sleep . . . us:* ready yourself for sleep, and you can listen to us laugh.

197. *omit . . . heavy offer:* overlook the offer of a deep, heavy sleep.

Sebastian   Why
Doth it not then our eyelids sink? I find not
Myself disposed to sleep.   205

Antonio   Nor I: my spirits are nimble.
They fell together all, as by consent.
They dropped as by a thunder-stroke. What might,
Worthy Sebastian — O, what might? — No more!
And yet methinks I see it in thy face,
What thou shouldst be. Th' occasion speaks thee,   210
    and
My strong imagination sees a crown
Dropping upon thy head.

Sebastian   What? Art thou waking?

Antonio Do you not hear me speak?

Sebastian   I do; and surely
It is a sleepy language, and thou speak'st
Out of thy sleep. What is it thou didst say?   215
This is a strange repose, to be asleep
With eyes wide open; standing, speaking, moving,
And yet so fast asleep.

Antonio   Noble Sebastian,
Thou let'st thy fortune sleep — die, rather; wink'st
Whiles thou art waking.   220

Sebastian   Thou dost snore distinctly;
There's meaning in thy snores.

Antonio I am more serious than my custom. You
Must be so too, if heed me; which to do
Trebles thee o'er.

Sebastian   Well, I am standing water.

Antonio I'll teach you how to flow.   225

Sebastian   Do so. To ebb
Hereditary sloth instructs me.

Antonio   O,
If you but knew how you the purpose cherish
Whiles thus you mock it! how, in stripping it,
You more invest it! Ebbing men indeed
(Most often) do so near the bottom run   230
By their own fear or sloth.

210. *th' occasion speaks thee:* the situation calls to you to take advantage of it.

212. *Art thou waking?:* i.e., perhaps you too have fallen asleep and are now dreaming.

219. *wink'st:* you keep your eyes shut as if asleep.

222. *than my custom:* than is customary with me.

224. *trebles thee o'er:* makes you three times greater than you are now.

standing water: i.e., as a tide standing still, between ebbing and flowing.

225–226. *To ebb . . . me:* as the second brother, Sebastian suggests, it is against his nature to be ambitious.

227–229. *If you but knew . . . .:* Antonio suggests that Sebastian secretly does desire to be king; "ebbing men," or men who move backwards in submission, never rise because of either fear or laziness.

Sebastian　　　　　　　Prithee say on.
The setting of thine eye and cheek proclaim
A matter from thee, and a birth, indeed,
Which throes thee much to yield.

Antonio　　　　　　　Thus, sir:
Although this lord of weak remembrance, this　235
Who shall be of as little memory
When he is earthed, hath here almost persuaded
(For he's a spirit of persuasion, only
Professes to persuade) the King his son's alive,
'Tis as impossible that he's undrowned　240
As he that sleeps here swims.

Sebastian　　　　　　　I have no hope
That he's undrowned.

Antonio　　　　　　　O, out of that no hope
What great hope have you! No hope that way is
Another way so high a hope that even
Ambition cannot pierce a wink beyond,　245
But doubt discovery there. Will you grant with me
That Ferdinand is drowned?

Sebastian　　　　　　　He's gone.

Antonio　　　　　　　Then tell me,
Who's the next heir of Naples?

Sebastian　　　　　　　Claribel.

Antonio She that is Queen of Tunis; she that
dwells
Ten leagues beyond man's life; she that from Naples　250
Can have no note, unless the sun were post —
The man i' th' moon's too slow — till newborn chins
Be rough and razorable; she that from whom
We all were sea-swallowed, though some cast again,
And, by that destiny, to perform an act　255
Whereof what's past is prologue, what to come,
Is yours and my discharge.

Sebastian　　　　　　　What stuff is this? How say you?
'Tis true my brother's daughter's Queen of Tunis;
So is she heir of Naples; 'twixt which regions
There is some space.　260

232. *setting:* fixed expression.
233. *A matter:* i.e., of importance.
234. *throes thee much:* causes you great pain.
235. *weak remembrance:* poor memory; meaning Gonzalo.
236. *as little memory:* as little remembered.
237. *earthed:* buried.
241–242. *no hope . . . undrowned:* i.e., I hope he is drowned.
242–246. *O, out of that . . . there:* With Ferdinand dead (so they suppose), Sebastian is next in line to the throne; if they can murder Alonso and get away with it, Sebastian will realize his wildest dreams.
245. *wink:* glimpse, view briefly.
250. *Ten leagues . . . life:* i.e., it would take more than a lifetime to get there. Antonio exaggerates: Tunis is only about 300 miles from Naples.
251. *note:* communication.
post.: messenger.
254. *cast again:* spit back by the sea.
256. *Whereof what's . . . prologue:* i.e., what has happened has prepared the setting for our act.
257. *discharge:* responsibility.

Antonio   A space whose ev'ry cubit
Seems to cry out "How shall that Claribel
Measure us back to Naples? Keep in Tunis,
And let Sebastian wake!" Say this were death,
That now hath seized them, why, they were no worse
Than now they are. There be that can rule Naples   265
As well as he that sleeps; lords that can prate
As amply and unnecessarily
As this Gonzalo; I myself could make
A chough of as deep chat. O, that you bore
The mind that I do! What a sleep were this   270
For your advancement! Do you understand me?

Sebastian Methinks I do.

Antonio   And how does your content
Tender your own good fortune?

Sebastian   I remember
You did supplant your brother Prospero.

Antonio   True.
And look how well my garments sit upon me,   275
Much feater than before. My brother's servants
Were then my fellows; now they are my men.

Sebastian But, for your conscience —

Antonio Ay sir, where lies that? If 'twere a kibe
'Twould put me to my slipper; but I feel not   280
This deity in my bosom. Twenty consciences
That stand 'twixt me and Milan, candied be they
And melt, ere they molest ! Here lies your brother,
No better than the earth he lies upon
If he were that which now he's like — that's dead;   285
Whom I with this obedient steel (three inches of it)
Can lay to bed for ever; whiles you, doing thus,
To the perpetual wink for aye might put
This ancient morsel, this Sir Prudence, who
Should not upbraid our course. For all the rest,   290
They'll take suggestion as a cat laps milk;
They'll tell the clock to any business that
We say befits the hour.

Sebastian   Thy case, dear friend,
Shall be my precedent. As thou got'st Milan,

262.   *us:* the cubits.

     Keep: addressed to Claribel.

265.   *There be:* There be those.

268–269. *Make . . . chough . . . chat:* teach a crow to speak as well, or with as much sense.

272–273. *And how . . . fortune?:* i.e., how do you feel about this opportunity to better yourself?

276.   *feater:* more gracefully.

277.   *fellows:* equals.

     men: servants.

279–280. *If 'twere . . . slipper:* if my heel had frostbite, I would be forced to wear my slippers (i.e., it is not as much trouble to me as a minor physical ailment).

282–283. *candied . . . melt:* let them dissolve, like sugared candy.

     molest: interfere.

286.   *this obedient steel:* my sword.

288.   *perpetual wink:* endless sleep; death.

     for aye: likewise.

289.   *ancient morsel:* old flesh; i.e., Gonzalo.

291.   *take suggestion:* act on an offered temptation.

292.   *tell . . . hour:* i.e., agree to whatever we say.

I'll come by Naples. Draw thy sword. One stroke   295
Shall free thee from the tribute which thou payest,
And I the King shall love thee.

Antonio   Draw together;
And when I rear my hand, do you the like,
To fall it on Gonzalo. [*They draw.*]

Sebastian   O, but one word!

Enter ARIEL [*invisible*] *with music and song.*

Ariel My master through his art forsees the danger   300
That you, his friend, are in, and sends me forth
(For else his project dies) to keep them living.

Sings in GONZALO'S *ear.*
While you here do snoring lie,
Open-eyed conspiracy
His time doth take.   305
If of life you keep a care,
Shake off slumber and beware.
Awake, awake!

Antonio Then let us both be sudden.

Gonzalo [*Wakes*]   Now good angels
Preserve the King!   310

Alonso Why, how now? — Ho, awake! — Why are
you drawn?
Wherefore this ghastly looking?

Gonzalo   What's the matter?

Sebastian Whiles we stood here securing your
repose,
Even now, we heard a hollow burst of bellowing
Like bulls, or rather lions. Did't not wake you?   315
It struck mine ear most terribly.

Alonso   I heard nothing.

Antonio O, 'twas a din to fright a monster's ear,
To make an earthquake! Sure it was the roar
Of a whole herd of lions.

Alonso   Heard you this, Gonzalo?

Gonzalo Upon mine honor, sir, I heard a humming,   320
And that a strange one too, which did awake me.

296. *the tribute:* money paid to the king (see I.2.113).

299. *but one word!:* one word more.

301–302. *That you . . . living:* Ariel speaks first to Gonzalo ("you") and then to the audience ("to keep them living").

304. *Open-eyed:* in contrast to the sleeping Gonzalo.

309. *sudden:* quick.

311. *drawn:* with swords drawn.
      Wherefore . . . looking?: i.e., why do you look frightened?

313. *securing:* watching over, guarding.

319. *herd of lions:* meant to expose the obviousness of Antonio's lies.

320. *a humming:* Ariel's song.

I shaked you sir, and cried. As mine eyes opened,
I saw their weapons drawn. There was a noise,
That's verily. 'Tis best we stand upon our guard,
Or that we quit this place. Let's draw our weapons.   325

Alonso Lead off this ground, and let's make further search
For my poor son.

Gonzalo   Heavens keep him from these beasts!
For he is sure I' th' island.   330

Alonso   Lead away.

Ariel Prospero my lord shall know what I have done.
So, King, go safely on to seek thy son. *Exeunt.*

COMMENTARY

The *protasis* or introduction of characters and scene continues through Act II. In this first scene of the act, we witness the court party, now cast ashore on the island. The process of understanding their similarities and differences, begun in the opening shipwreck scene and hinted at through Prospero's references to three of these characters (Gonzalo, Antonio, and Alonso) in his story, is here furthered and clarified.

Gonzalo is clearly recognizable as the noble counselor who served as the agent of divine providence in outfitting Prospero and the infant Miranda, with food, fresh water, and books for their enforced

"Gonzalo: How lush and lusty the grass looks! how green! Antonio: The ground, indeed, is tawny" (II.1.51–52). Different characters seem to see and experience the island in different ways. To some it is desolate and unattractive, to others it is almost a paradise. Individual characters' attitudes toward situation and setting suggest either the villainy or nobility of that character in several instances.
Gemaldegalerie, Dresden, Germany/A.K.G., Berlin/SuperStock

sea journey. Gonzalo persistently sees the world in optimistic terms. To him, and to Adrian, a minor lord with similarly positivistic tendencies, the air breathes sweetly and the island has a great deal of beauty with which to recommend itself. It is a miracle they are alive and unhurt; even their clothes are as fresh, he asserts, as when they first put them on for Claribel's wedding. All of this is, however, of cold comfort to Alonso, who believes his son is drowned.

Antonio and Sebastian stand removed from the remainder of the court party and look at the scene and circumstances with a far more cynical and negative view. To them, the island air smells not of sweet perfume but of a fen or a swamp; they consider the island barren and "tawny," not green; they judge their clothes stained, their situation lamentable.

This is perhaps a sophisticated play on the idea of a "desert" island. Not only is the island a desert in that it is sparsely populated; it is an island ruled by desert, by what one deserves. That is, good people see and experience good in the island, while bad people see and experience negativity.

Gonzalo is well-meaning, if also somewhat foolish. An example of this comes in the clash he and Antonio have over his term "Widow Dido." Dido, the Queen of Carthage who fell in love with Aeneas (according to Virgil in the *Aeneid)*, the eventual forefather of Rome, was indeed a widow although this aspect of her character is rarely stressed. Tunis and Carthage are not literally the same city, but in certain respects Gonzalo is right that, after the destruction of Carthage, Tunis became the center of trade and politics in Northern Africa. The two cities were physically separate, but by a distance of only a few miles.

Francisco, another minor character, jumps in at this point, likewise trying to comfort the King, and suggests that Ferdinand proved stronger than the raging ocean and came alive to shore. Alonso wallows in self pity, however, and cannot be persuaded from his belief that Ferdinand is forever lost. Sebastian speaks the truth but harshly suggesting to the King that all his woes are his own fault.

Gonzalo tries a different tactic to cheer up the King, speaking of the island and how he would manage it were he its king. It is here that Shakespeare reveals his close reading of Florio's translation of Montaigne; Gonzalo's speech echoes word for word several passages from Montaigne's description of the organization of the cannibal nation as one

> that hath no kind of traffic, no knowledge of letters, no intelligence of numbers, no name of magistrate, nor of politic superiority; no use of service, of riches or of poverty; no contracts, no successions, no partitions, no occupation but idle; no respect of kindred, but common, no apparel but natural, no manuring of lands, no use of wine, corn, or mettle. The very words that import lying, falsehood, treason, dissimulation, covetousness, envy, detraction, and pardon, were never heard of amongst them.... (*The Complete Essays of Montaigne*, trans. Donald M. Frame. Stanford, 1957).

Gonzalo believes in the inherent goodness of man and in the power of nature. The scene he describes is that of a Golden Age, an age in which reason and goodness triumph over selfishness, greed, and envy. This is, in fact, how Gonzalo sees the world. Not everyone on the island agrees with him, however, and the earlier contradictory points of view of Gonzalo against Antonio and Sebastian may be merely a difference of opinion; but they might also be a product of Prospero's magic wherein different individuals experience different forms of reality on the island, each according to his temperament and desert.

While Gonzalo clearly agrees with Montaigne's position, Shakespeare may not. As counter to the praise Montaigne affords the savage cannibals, Shakespeare presents Caliban as a would-be rapist, murderer, and revolutionary. However, as noted earlier and as will soon be seen, Caliban is not a simple brute; although he claims that the principal good to come of his learning language is the ability to curse, we will shortly witness him using language for far more lyrical purposes.

Ariel enters and charms the court party, except for Antonio and Sebastian, into sleep, according to Prospero's command. Prospero's design is to test Antonio and Sebastian, although he is confident of what action this opportunity will prompt these two to take. Antonio and Sebastian do not disappoint Prospero and see the strange sleep that falls on Alonso and Gonzalo as the perfect opportunity to murder them and steal more political power for themselves. Antonio in particular emerges as cold-blooded and ruthless, confirming the report of him we received from Prospero in Act I, Scene 2. He follows in a grand tradition of exquisite Shakespearean villains stretching from Richard III to Edmund in *King Lear*, Iago in *Othello*, and the eponymous tragic hero of *Macbeth*. Like these famous villains, Antonio is without a moral center; if, in Prospero's study of the spiritual world, he has an excess of spirituality, his brother Antonio balances this by having none.

Antonio and Sebastian's utter lack of graciousness toward Gonzalo is a further clue to their characters. Both Antonio and Sebastian suffer from an excess of pride and self-righteousness. They have neither time nor patience for Gonzalo, whom they judge to be old and infirm. Take note of the terms with which they refer to him in this scene: "old cock," "lord of weak remembrance," "ancient morsel." Their vision of Gonzalo is that of a weak old man. Prospero in the previous scene describes Gonzalo as noble, and tells Miranda that it was only through his kindness that they (Prospero and Miranda) did not die when kicked out of Milan and cast out to sea in a leaky boat. The lack of charity with which Antonio and Sebastian view Gonzalo, the character presented as perhaps the most noble and charitable figure in the play, is a clear indication that Antonio and Sebastian suffer from a consuming corruption of character.

As Antonio and Sebastian prepare to steep themselves in blood, Ariel returns and awakens the sleepers, beginning with Gonzalo. Exposed for their treachery, Antonio and Sebastian attempt to lie their way out of it but make a mess of doing so. It is a deliberate mistake on Shakespeare's part that Antonio describes the nonexistent noise that led him and Sebastian to draw their swords as coming from "a herd" (rather than a pride) of lions. With subtle humor on Shakespeare's part, Gonzalo describes this supposed din or thunderous noise as a strange "humming." Sebastian and Antonio have just gone to great lengths to describe the noises that awoke the sleeping King as having been produced by bulls or lions — a thunderous noise. Gonzalo does not accuse them of being liars (he is far too gracious for that) but instead describes what he heard as a "humming," the opposite, in other words, of the quality and volume of noise Antonio and Sebastian claim to have heard. The audience witnessed no such noise; we heard only Ariel's song. That Antonio and Sebastian are lying — and lying badly — is further suggested when Antonio (who prides himself on his cleverness) makes the mistake of describing a pride of lions as a herd.

Act II, Scene 2

Caliban fears that Prospero's magical servants are watching and intending to torture him for being a bad servant; he hides underneath his own cloak. Trinculo, the King's jester, fears that a storm is coming and seeks shelter from it underneath Caliban's cloak. Stephano, drunk on wine, discovers both of them and shares his wine with them. Caliban, intoxicated by his first taste of alcohol, promises to worship and serve Stephano.

ACT II, SCENE 2.
[Another part of the island.]

Enter CALIBAN *with a burden of wood. A noise of thunder heard.*

Caliban All the infections that the sun sucks up
From bogs, fens, flats, on Prosper fall, and make
   him
By inchmeal a disease! His spirits hear me,
And yet I needs must curse. But they'll nor pinch,
Fright me with urchin-shows, pitch me i' th' mire,   5
Nor lead me, like a firebrand, in the dark
Out of my way, unless he bid 'em; but
For every trifle are they set upon me;
Sometime like apes that mow and chatter at me,
And after bite me; then like hedgehogs which   10
Lie tumbling in my barefoot way and mount
Their pricks at my footfall; sometime am I
All wound with adders, who with cloven tongues
Do hiss me into madness.

Enter TRINCULO.
                     Lo, now, lo!
Here comes a spirit of his, and to torment me   15
For bringing wood in slowly. I'll fall flat.
Perchance he will not mind me. [*Lies down.*]

Trinculo Here's neither bush nor shrub to bear off
any weather at all, and another storm brewing: I
hear it sing i' th' wind. Yond same black cloud, yond   20
huge one, looks like a foul bombard that would shed
his liquor. If it should thunder as it did before, I
know not where to hide my head. Yond same cloud
cannot choose but fall by pailfuls. What have we

NOTES

3.   *By inchmeal:* inch by inch.

4.   *nor:* neither.

5.   *urchin-shows:* visions of goblins in the forms of hedgehogs.

6.   *like a firebrand:* like a flaming torch or the will-o'-the-wisp (see Commentary).

8.   *every trifle:* the smallest reason.

9.   *mow:* make faces.

13.   *All wound:* twined about with.

     cloven: forked

17.   *mind:* notice.

18.   *bear off:* protect me from.

21.   *bombard:* both a type of cannon and a large leather jug. Trinculo plays on both meanings.

here? a man or a fish? dead or alive? A fish: he 25
smells like a fish; a very ancient and fishlike smell;
a kind of not of the newest poor-John. A strange fish!
Were I in England now, as once I was, and had but
this fish painted, not a holiday fool there but would
give a piece of silver. There would this monster 30
make a man: any strange beast there makes a man
When they will not give a doit to relieve a lame beggar, they will lay out ten to see a dead Indian.
Legged like a man! and his fins like arms! Warm, o'
my troth! I do now let loose my opinion, hold it no 35
longer: this is no fish, but an islander, that hath
lately suffered by a thunderbolt. [*Thunder.*] Alas,
the storm is come again! My best way is to creep
under his gaberdine: there is no other shelter here-
about. Misery acquaints a man with strange bed- 40
fellows. I will here shroud till the dregs of the storm
be past. [*Creeps under* CALIBAN'S *garment.*]

Enter STEPHANO *singing* [*a bottle in his hand.*]

Stephano I shall no more to sea, to sea;
        Here shall I die ashore.
This is a very scurvy tune to sing at a man's funeral. 45
Well, here's my' comfort. (*Drinks* [*then*] *Sings.*)
        The master, the swabber, the boatswain, and I,
           The gunner, and his mate,
        Loved Mall, Meg, and Marian, and Margery,
           But none of us cared for Kate. 50
           For she had a tongue with a tang,
           Would cry to a sailor "Go hang!"
        She loved not the savor of tar nor of pitch;
        Yet a tailor might scratch her wher'er she did
           itch.
           Then to sea, boys, and let her go hang! 55
This is a scurvy tune too; but here's my comfort. (*Drinks.*)

Caliban Do not torment me! O!

Stephano What's the matter? Have we devils here?
Do you put tricks upon 's with savages and men of
Inde, ha? I have not scaped drowning to be 60
afeard now of your four legs; for it hath been said,

27. *poor-John:* dried, salted fish.

29. *painted:* painted on a sign outside a booth at a fair.

31. *make:* earn money for.

32. *doit:* small coin of little value.

33. *a dead indian:* Shakespeare's audience was fascinated with the New World native people. Dead or alive, they made popular attractions at the fairs.

39. *gaberdine:* cloak.

41. *dregs:* last drops, bottom of the barrel.

47. *swabber:* sailor who mops or "swabs" the ship's decks.

53. *tar . . . pitch:* associated with sailors.

54. *a tailor:* members of this trade were considered effeminate, and thus the suggestion here is that "Kate" was easily satisified sexually.

59–60. *men of Inde:* Indians.

"As proper a man as ever went on four legs cannot
make him give ground"; and it shall be said so
again, while Stephano breathes at nostrils.

Caliban The spirit torments me. O!   65

Stephano This is some monster of the isle, with
four legs, who hath got, as I take it, an ague. Where
the devil should he learn our language? I will give
him some relief, if it be but for that. If I can recover him, and keep him tame, and get to Naples   70
with him, he's a present for any emperor that ever
trod on neat's leather.

Caliban Do not torment me, prithee; I'll bring my
wood home faster.

Stephano He's in his fit now and does not talk   75
after the wisest. He shall taste of my bottle: if he
have never drunk wine afore, it will go near to remove his fit. If I can recover him and keep him
tame, I will not take too much for him; he shall pay
for him that hath him, and that soundly.   80

Caliban Thou dost me yet but little hurt.
Thou wilt anon; I know it by thy trembling.
Now Prosper works upon thee.

Stephano Come on your ways: open your mouth:
here is that which will give language to you, cat.   85
Open your mouth. This will shake your shaking, I
can tell you, and that soundly. [*Gives* CALIBAN *drink*.]
You cannot tell who's your friend. Open your
chaps again.

Trinculo I should know that voice. It should be —   90
but he is drowned; and these are devils. O, defend
me!

Stephano Four legs and two voices — a most delicate monster! His forward voice now is to speak
well of his friend; his backward voice is to utter   95
foul speeches and to detract. If all the wine in my
bottle will recover him, I will help his ague. Come!
[*Gives drink*.] Amen! I will pour some in thy other
mouth.

62. *four legs:* Stephano's confused modification of the proverb "As proper a man as ever went on two legs. . . ."

64. *at nostrils:* through the nose.

67. *ague:* feverish shivers or shakes.

72. *neat's leather:* cowhide.

76. *after the wisest:* with much sense or intelligence.

79. *too much:* i.e., all I can get.

82. *anon:* soon.

85. *cat:* reference to the proverb "Liquor will make a cat talk."

89. *chaps:* jaws.

Trinculo Stephano!   100

Stephano Doth thy other mouth call me? Mercy, mercy! This is a devil, and no monster. I will leave him; I have no long spoon.

Trinculo Stephano! If thou beest Stephano, touch me and speak to me; for I am Trinculo — be not   105 afeard — thy good friend Trinculo.

Stephano If thou beest Trinculo, come forth. I'll pull thee by the lesser legs. If any be Trinculo's legs, these are they.

[*Draws him out from under* CALIBAN'S *garment.*]
Thou art very Trinculo indeed: how cam'st thou to   110 be the siege of this mooncalf? Can he vent Trinculos?

Trinculo I took him to be killed with a thunder-stroke. But art thou not drowned, Stephano? I hope now thou art not drowned. Is the storm overblown? I hid me under the dead mooncalf's gaberdine for   115 fear of the storm. And art thou living, Stephano? O Stephano, two Neapolitans scaped!

Stephano Prithee do not turn me about: my stomach is not constant.

Caliban [*Aside*] These be fine things, an if they be   120 not sprites.
That's a brave god and bears celestial liquor.
I will kneel to him.

Stephano How didst thou scape? How cam'st thou hither? Swear by this bottle how thou cam'st hither.   125 I escaped upon a butt of sack which the sailors heaved o'erboard, by this bottle, which I made of the bark of a tree with mine own hands since I was cast ashore.

Caliban I'll swear upon that bottle to be thy true   130 subject, for the liquor is not earthly.

Stephano Here! Swear then how thou escapedst.

Trinculo Swum ashore, man, like a duck. I can swim like a duck, I'll be sworn.

103. *long spoon:* reference to the proverb "He who sups with the devil must have a long spoon."

111. *siege:* excrement.
mooncalf: monstrosity.
vent: defecate.

114. *overblown:* blown over, passed.

117. *Neapolitans:* people from Naples

120. *an if:* if.

126. *butt of sack:* barrel of white wine imported from Spain and the Canary Islands; also referred to as "canary" and "sherry."

Stephano Here, kiss the book. [*Gives him drink.*]   135
Though thou canst swim like a duck, thou art made
like a goose.

Trinculo O Stephano, hast any more of this?

Stephano The whole butt, man: my cellar is in a
rock by th' seaside, where my wine is hid. How   140
now, mooncalf? How does thine ague?

Caliban Hast thou not dropped from heaven?

Stephano Out o' th' moon, I do assure thee. I was
the Man i' th' Moon when time was.

Caliban I have seen thee in her, and I do adore   145
thee.
My mistress showed me thee, and thy dog, and thy
bush.

Stephano Come, swear to that; kiss the book. I
will furnish it anon with new contents. Swear.

[CALIBAN *drinks*.]

Trinculo By this good light, this is a very shallow
monster! I afeard of him A very weak monster!   150
The Man i' th' Moon? A most poor credulous monster! — Well drawn, monster, in good sooth!

Caliban I'll show thee every fertile inch o' th'
island;
And I will kiss thy foot. I prithee be my god.   155

Trinculo By this light, a most perfidious and
drunken monster! When god's asleep, he'll rob his
bottle.

Caliban I'll kiss thy foot. I'll swear myself thy
subject.

Stephano Come on then. Down, and swear!

Trinculo I shall laugh myself to death at this   160
puppy-headed monster. A most scurvy monster! I
could find in my heart to beat him —

Stephano Come, kiss.

Trinculo But that the poor monster's in drink. An
abominable monster!   165

---

135. *kiss the book:* i.e., the bottle; Caliban regards Stephano as a god, and the performance is a parody of a religious ceremony, with the bottle as a sacred book (see Commentary).

137. *goose:* with a long neck, meaning a long draw from the bottle. Possibly also a "silly goose."

144. *when time was:* once upon a time.

146. *dog . . . bush:* legend held that a man was banished to the moon for gathering firewood on the sabbath (see Commentary).

149. *shallow:* simple, stupid.

151. *credulous:* gullible.

152. *Well drawn:* well drunk.

155. *'perfidious:* treacherous, not to be trusted.

Caliban I'll show thee the best springs; I'll pluck
    thee berries;
I'll fish for thee, and get thee wood enough.
A plague upon the tyrant that I serve!
I'll bear him no more sticks, but follow thee,
Thou wondrous man.   170

Trinculo A most ridiculous monster, to make a
wonder of a poor drunkard!

Caliban I prithee let me bring thee where crabs
    grow;
And I with my long nails will dig thee pignuts,
Show thee a jay's nest, and instruct thee how   175
To snare the nimble marmoset; I'll bring thee
To clust'ring filberts, and sometimes I'll get thee
Young scamels from the rock. Wilt thou go with me?

Stephano I prithee now, lead the way without any
more talking. Trinculo, the King and all our com-   180
pany else being drowned, we will inherit here. Here,
bear my bottle. Fellow Trinculo, we'll fill him by
and by again.

[CALIBAN *sings drunkenly.*]

Caliban Farewell, master; farewell, farewell!

Trinculo A howling monster! a drunken monster!   185

Caliban No more dams I'll make for fish.
           No fetch in firing,
            At requiring,
      Nor scrape trenchers, nor wash dish.
          'Ban, 'Ban. Ca-Caliban   190
          Has a new master, get a new man.
Freedom, high-day! high-day, freedom! freedom,
high-day, freedom!

Stephano O brave monster! lead the way. *Exeunt.*

---

173.   *crabs:* shellfish or, possibly, crab apples.

174.   *pignuts:* bitter nuts of the pignut tree.

176.   *marmoset:* a small monkey.

177.   *filberts:* hazelnuts.

178.   *scamels:* an unknown word; probably a misprint for sea-mell or sea-mew, a rock-nesting bird.

181.   *we will inherit:* we will take complete possession.

187.   *firing:* firewood.

189.   *scrape trenchers nor wash dish:* scrape clean trenchers (wooden plates) or wash dishes.

191.   *high-day:* liberty, holiday.

      get a new man: i.e., Prospero needs to find a new servant to do his chores.

COMMENTARY

With this scene, the tone of *The Tempest* changes considerably. Caliban appears almost vulnerable in his opening lines of complaint and paranoia. In his version of events, Prospero is an unrelenting taskmaster who uses his control over magic spirits to extract hard labor from Caliban. Any resistance is met with torture (fevers and cramps). Notice that throughout this scene Caliban speaks in *verse* (metered poetry), while Stephano and Trinculo speak in prose. For the most part in Shakespeare's plays, verse is spoken by Kings and noble characters, while the comic characters and characters of lower social standing speak in prose. Caliban's lines in this scene suggest that the language instruction Prospero and Miranda provided him left him with more than just the ability to curse.

When Caliban refers to the torments that Prospero's spirits plague him with as "like a firebrand" he is likely referring to what is known as the "Will o' the Wisp." This phenomenon, which is known under the Latin name of *Ignis Fatuus* or "fool's fire," is "a flame-like phosphorescence flitting over marshy ground (due to the spontaneous combustion of gases from decaying vegetable matter [swamp gas, in other words]) and deluding people who attempt to follow it; hence any delusive aim or object (a "wild goose chase") or some Utopian scheme that is utterly impracticable" (*Brewer's Dictionary of Phrase and Fable*, 14th edition. New York: Harper & Row, 1989). Caliban is certainly prone to such fantasies; strikingly, the other character in the play who exhibits passionate idealism, and goes so far as to describe his own (impractical and impracticable) Utopia, is Gonzalo.

When Caliban hears the thunder overhead, it frightens him not as a warning of oncoming storm but as a reminder of Prospero's threatening voice; he interprets the thunder as a sign that Prospero's magical spirits ("Ariel and all his quality") have heard his complaints and are coming to punish him for bringing his wood home so slowly. He mistakes Trinculo for one of those spirits — a comic inversion of the romantic exchange at the end of Act I, Scene 2, in which Miranda and Ferdinand mistake one another for spiritual or divine beings.

Trinculo is readily recognizable as a stock comic character, the court jester, through his parti-colored clothes. Although a comic character, everything Trinculo says is not to be seen as immediately funny. Instead, it is in the interaction and often grandly bumbling actions of Trinculo, Stephano, and Caliban that the comedy emerges. Trinculo is nervous and scares easily and, as a result, both Stephano and Caliban bully him.

Trinculo, unlike Caliban, seeks shelter from the rainstorm that the thunderous sound effects forewarn. The only shelter available to him is the strange lump of cloth that is Caliban cowering underneath his cloak. Despite the foulness of Caliban's smell — like that of old fish — Trinculo crawls underneath his gaberdine to create the appearance of a four-legged, two-headed beast.

"Sometime am I all wound with adders, who with cloven tongues / Do hiss me into madness" (II.2.13–14). Caliban complains bitterly of the torments Prospero visits upon him for his negative attitude toward service. Prospero manipulates nature to torment Caliban rather than torturing him with devils or demons.
Musee de Louvre, Paris/SuperStock

It is this beast that the drunken butler, Stephano, stumbles upon as he enters while singing drinking songs that would undoubtedly get him into considerable trouble in polite company. His songs are sailors' songs, leading some to believe that he is the ship's butler rather than one of Alonzo's household servants. Where he worked before matters little. What matters now is that he is drunk — remaining so throughout the play — and in possession of a barrel of wine and a bottle that he very proudly has made with his own hands.

"What have we here? A man or a fish?" (II.2.25). Caliban is a mysterious creature and one that has often fascinated and challenged actors and designers. The figure shown here, based on a sixteenth-century encyclopedia illustration, gives some hint to his strangeness. Trinculo claims that he is half fish and later in the play, Alonso proclaims Caliban as "strange a thing as e'er [he] looked on" (V.1.289).

Stephano is an unlikely choice to overthrow Prospero as ruler of the island, but he is Caliban's choice nonetheless (after Caliban gets a taste of the contents of Stephano's bottle). Liquor proves a magical elixir indeed to Caliban. Caliban, inspired by his first-ever taste of wine, pledges allegiance to Stephano and promises to show him all the natural treasures of the island. Listen here for echoes of Caliban's account of his first meetings with Prospero as described in Act I, Scene 2.

Caliban mistakes both Stephano and Trinculo first as spirits and later as gods. Stephano is a vivid braggart, proclaiming himself the man in the moon. Legend held that the man in the moon — who is pictured always with his faithful dog and a bundle of twigs (Shakespeare also drew on this familiar figure for his comic scenes in *A Midsummer Night's Dream*) — was banished to the moon for gathering firewood on the Sabbath. Thus, Stephano sets himself up, unknowingly, as a wittily ironic god for Caliban to worship, because it is Caliban's job to fetch in firewood and, unlike the man in the moon who would do so even on a day of rest, Caliban only ever undertakes this task with grumbling and complaint.

Comedy arises naturally out of character and situation here, as these three bumblers hatch a plan to take over the island. Shakespeare may well be poking fun at English Catholics by having Stephano refer to his bottle as a "book" and encouraging both Caliban and Trinculo to "kiss the book." Touching one's lips to the Bible, and specifically the Gospel or New Testament, was a form of religious ritual, presented here as laughable; although not exclusively, this was an aspect of Roman Catholic ritual. Caliban's discovery of the power of liquor is a mock-conversion to a new "religion" and, thus, Stephano is in part a mockery of European colonial missionaries. Although the New World colonizers were both Protestant and Catholic, the Roman Catholic Spanish were far more involved in colonization as both a mercantile and a religious enterprise than any other European nation. The transformative power of wine — here in a degrading sense — among this unholy trinity may be a larger project of mocking the Catholic doctrine of transubstantiation, in which it was believed that the bread and wine used in the Eucharistic supper or Communion literally *became* the flesh and blood of Jesus Christ. Trinculo comments on the ridiculousness of Caliban's behavior, but the drunkenness of the scene quickly sweeps such skepticism aside and all three characters exit in high spirits to the accompaniment of Caliban's song.

In addition to the likely mockery of religion at work in this scene, there is also, clearly, a subtle mockery of Prospero's magic. Caliban sees Trinculo, and especially Stephano, as gods, and he sees the liquor that Stephano gives to Caliban as "celestial," or from heaven. In addition to this being an inversion of the first meeting of Ferdinand and Miranda, it is also a mockery of Prospero's magic. The taste of Stephano's wine is a magical, transcendental experience for Caliban and, as a result of it, he swiftly pledges allegiance to the butler. Dissatisfied as he was with serving Prospero, this is not surprising. Little does Caliban know that for all his fear of the cramps and other physical pains Prospero inflicts on him, his new master (drink) will prove equally if not more painful. Caliban and his compatriots (Stephano and Trinculo) realize this by the play's conclusion and admit to their own folly in the play's final scene.

The construction of this scene is remarkably neat. It picks up in pace with the entrance of Stephano, who is engaged in drunken song. By the close of the scene, all three characters are well on their way to drunkenness, and the festive singing overtakes the entire happy band.

"When the will not give a doit to relieve a lame beggar, the will lay out ten to see a dead Indian" (II.2.32–34). Trinculo makes reference to the fascination Early Modern Britons held for what they considered curiosities, including natives from foreign lands — especially the New World. This illustration is based on one produced by Inigo Jones for The Masque of the Middle Temple and Lincoln's Inn *in 1613 (thus, just a few years after the first performance of* The Tempest*). It is one example of the use of Indians and other "strange" natives in popular entertainment.*

Notes

THE TEMPEST
ACT III

Caliban *Be not afeared: the isle is full of noises,*
Sounds and sweet airs that give delight and hurt not.
Sometimes a thousand twangling instruments
Will hum about my ears; and sometimes voices
That, if I then had waked after long sleep,
Will make me sleep again; and then, in dreaming,
The clouds methought would open and show riches
Ready to drop upon me, that, when I waked,
I cried to dream again.

Act III, Scene 1

Ferdinand piles firewood as commanded by Prospero. Miranda attempts to assist him. Prospero, unseen by the young lovers, watches with delight as their affection for one another grows and they proclaim their love.

ACT III, Scene 1.
[Before Prospero's cell.]

Enter FERDINAND, *bearing a log.*

Ferdinand There be some sports are painful, and
    their labor
Delight in them sets off; some kinds of baseness
Are nobly undergone, and most poor matters
Point to rich ends. This my mean task
Would be as heavy to me as odious, but   5
The mistress which I serve quickens what's dead
And makes my labors pleasures. O, she is
Ten times more gentle than her father's crabbed;
And he's composed of harshness! I must remove
Some thousands of these logs and pile them up,   10
Upon a sore injunction. My sweet mistress
Weeps when she sees me work, and says such baseness
Had never like executor. I forget;
But these sweet thoughts do even refresh my labors
Most busy least, when I do it.   15

Enter MIRANDA *and* PROSPERO [*behind, unseen.*]

Miranda   Alas, now pray you
Work not so hard! I would the lightning had
Burnt up those logs that you are enjoined to pile!
Pray set it down and rest you. When this burns,
Some thousands of these logs and pile them up,
'Twill weep for having wearied you. My father
Is hard at study: pray now rest yourself.   20
He's safe for these three hours.

Ferdinand   O most dear mistress,
The sun will set before I shall discharge
What I must strive to do.

NOTES

1.   *painful:* difficult.

2.   *Delight . . . sets off:* The strain of certain sports makes their enjoyment greater.

     baseness: lowliness or embarrassment.

3.   *most poor. . . ends:* i.e., lowly duties lead to great results.

5.   *odious:* hateful.

6.   *quickens:* brings to life.

8.   *crabbed:* bad-tempered, crabby.

9.   *composed:* made of nothing but.

11. *sore injunction:* stern command.

12. *such baseness . . . executor:* such a lowly task was never done by one so noble.

14. *sweet thoughts:* i.e., of Miranda.

15. *Most busy . . . it:* i.e., when I am busy, I am least conscious of being busy (because of the "sweet thoughts").

19. *'Twill weep:* Miranda's fanciful term refers to water or resin oozing from the burning wood.

Miranda If you'll sit down,
I'll bear your logs the while. Pray give me that:
I'll carry it to the pile.   25

Ferdinand   No, precious creature:
I had rather crack my sinews, break my back,
Than you should such dishonor undergo
While I sit lazy by.

Miranda   It would become me
As well as it does you; and I should do it
With much more ease; for my good will is to it,   30
And yours it is against.

Prospero [*Aside*] Poor worm, thou art infected
This visitation shows it.

Miranda   You look wearily.

Ferdinand No, noble mistress: 'tis fresh morning
  with me
When you are by at night. I do beseech you,
Chiefly that I might set it in my prayers,   35
What is your name?

Miranda   Miranda. O my father,
I have broke your hest to say so!

Ferdinand   Admired Miranda!
Indeed the top of admiration, worth
What's dearest to the world! Full many a lady
I have eyed with best regard, and many a time   40
Th' harmony of their tongues hath into bondage
Brought my too diligent ear; for several virtues
Have I liked several women; never any
With so full soul but some defect in her
Did quarrel with the noblest grace she owed,   45
And put it to the foil. But you, O you,
So perfect and so peerless, are created
Of every creature's best.

Miranda   I do not know
One of my sex; no woman's face remember,
Save, from my glass, mine own; nor have I seen   50
More that I may call men than you, good friend,
And my dear father. How features are abroad
I am skilless of; but, by my modesty

28.	*become:* suit.
32.	*visitation:* visit, observation; possibly also in the sense of a visitation or outbreak of disease.
33–34.	*fresh . . . night:* Ferdinand's lines smack of exaggeration and smoothness; he suggests that Miranda, at first meeting, is the sunshine of his life.
37.	*hest:* command.
38.	*admiration:* wonder (see I.2.427).
40.	*best regard:* highest approval.
42.	*diligent ear:* i.e., listening closely.
43.	*several:* various.
44.	*With so full soul:* completely.
46.	*put . . . foil:* set it off by contrast; also, playing on "quarrel," to challenge.
48 ff.	Miranda speaks in direct contrast to Ferdinand's boast of knowing many women.
52.	*abroad:* elsewhere in the world.

(The jewel in my dower), I would not wish
Any companion in the world but you;   55
Nor can imagination form a shape,
Besides yourself, to like of. But I prattle
Something too wildly, and my father's precepts
I therein do forget.

Ferdinand   I am, in my condition,
A prince, Miranda; I do think, a king   60
(I would not so), and would no more endure
This wooden slavery than to suffer
The flesh fly blow my mouth. Hear my soul speak!
The very instant that I saw you, did
My heart fly to your service; there resides,   65
To make me slave to it; and for your sake
Am I this patient log-man.

Miranda   Do you love me?

Ferdinand O heaven, O earth, bear witness to this
      sound,
And crown what I profess with kind event
If I speak true! if hollowly, invert   70
What best is boded me to mischief! I,
Beyond all limit of what else i' th' world,
Do love, prize, honor you.

Miranda   I am a fool
To weep at what I am glad of.

Prospero [*Aside*]   Fair encounter
Of two most rare affections! Heavens rain grace   75
On that which breeds between 'em!

Ferdinand   Wherefore weep you?

Miranda At mine unworthiness, that dare not offer
What I desire to give, and much less take
What I shall die to want. But this is trifling;
And all the more it seeks to hide itself,   80
The bigger bulk it shows. Hence, bashful cunning,
And prompt me, plain and holy innocence!
I am your wife, if you will marry me;
If not, I'll die your maid. To be your fellow
You may deny me; but I'll be your servant,   85
Whether you will or no.

59. *condition:* rank in society.

63. *flesh fly:* bluebottle fly, which lays its eggs in rotting flesh.

blow: lay its eggs. Ferdinand uses this as a metaphor for the ultimate indignation or embarrassment.

69. *kind event:* a happy ending.

71. *is boded:* is in store for; i.e., punish me if I speak lies.

77. *dare not offer . . . :* i.e., Miranda longs to accept Ferdinand's offer of marriage and to offer herself in return, even if it is improper for her to do so.

79. *want:* lack.

81. *bashful cunning:* forced shyness.

84. *maid:* in the senses of (1) virgin, (2) servant (as in line 85).

fellow: partner.

Ferdinand   My mistress, dearest.
And I thus humble ever.

Miranda   My husband then?

Ferdinand Ay, with a heart as willing
As bondage e'er of freedom. Here's my hand.

Miranda And mine, with my heart in't; and now   90
farewell
Till half an hour hence.

Ferdinand   A thousand thousand!

Exeunt [FERDINAND *and* MIRANDA *severally*].

Prospero So glad of this as they I cannot be,
Who are surprised withal; but my rejoicing
At nothing can be more. I'll to my book;
For yet ere supper time must I perform   95
Much business appertaining. [*Exit.*]

89. *As bondage . . . freedom:* i.e., with as much desire as one who is in prison longs to be free.

91. *thousand thousand:* i.e., goodbyes of farewells.

93. *Who are surprised:* i.e., Ferdinand and Miranda, who were unaware of what was to happen to them.

96. *appertaining:* pertaining or related to the blossoming romance of Ferdinand and Miranda.

COMMENTARY

The invitation to compare and contrast Ferdinand with Caliban continues as this scene begins with a visual echo of the previous scene. Caliban began the previous scene carrying in a load of firewood and complaining bitterly about his enforced service to Prospero. Here Ferdinand enters, also carrying firewood in service to Prospero, but speaks less of his dislike for the present task than the reward that awaits his successful completion of it — marriage to Miranda. Ferdinand, in his opening speech, draws a comparison between his labor and painful sports ("No pain, no gain," in late-twentieth-century terms). As a seventeenth-century prince, Ferdinand is well versed in the rituals and language of courtly love, or chivalry. He understands the test Prospero is subjecting him to as a means of proving his loyalty, fidelity, and worth.

Ferdinand's knowledge of speaking with noble ladies also emerges in his conversation with Miranda. He is a bit of a pickup artist: practiced, smooth, and flattering in his use of language. Miranda, however, is direct and sensitive to the complexities of language. She certainly wants to believe him but senses at the same time that there appears some exaggeration in the head-over-heels love of which Ferdinand claims to be the victim.

Miranda pushes Ferdinand to answer to the promise of marriage directly. "My husband then?" she asks (line 88). Assured by his answer, they seal the deal with a handshake (not a kiss), a symbol of the purity and chastity of their love.

The central theme that is represented in the marriage of Ferdinand and Miranda is the redemption of the older generation by the children. The conflict and tensions between Alonso and Prospero are to be smoothed over through the marriage of their children. The theme of redemption of fathers (especially) through their children — and specifically daughters who redeem their fathers — runs through all of Shakespeare's late plays (the Romances) — *Pericles*, *Cymbeline*, *The Winter's Tale*, and *The Tempest*.

Prospero, who has observed the entire exchange between Miranda and Ferdinand unseen, is thrilled by the progress. A marriage between Ferdinand and Miranda, in addition to its romantic overtones, is also part of Prospero's political scheme. Their union represents a partnership, and shared government in the future of Milan and Naples. In the background story that Prospero tells in Act I, Scene 2, we learn that Alonso, the King of Naples, was instrumental in the rebellion that removed Prospero, the rightful Duke of Milan, from power. In other words, there has been political tension between the rightful ruling families of these two city-states. Prospero's hope for the future is that there can be peace. Part of his design to achieve that peace includes the uniting, through marriage, of his family with Alonso's.

As much as Prospero would like to rejoice over the successful progress of his plans thus far, the plot goes on, he reminds us; there is much business relative to Ferdinand and Miranda's future marriage, as well as Prospero's designs for revenge against Alonso and Antonio, to attend to before this play will be done.

Act III, Scene 2

Drink has fully seeped into the brains of Stephano, Caliban, and Trinculo. Stephano and Trinculo turn argumentative and begin to bicker with one another. Caliban proposes a plot to kill Prospero and make Stephano the king of the island; this plot is overheard by Ariel, who promises to report it to Prospero.

ACT III, SCENE 2.
[Another part of the island.]

Enter CALIBAN, STEPHANO, *and* TRINCULO.

Stephano Tell not me! When the butt is out, we
will drink water; not a drop before. Therefore bear
up, and board 'em! Servant monster, drink to me.

Trinculo Servant monster? The folly of this island!
They say there's but five upon this isle: we are   5
three of them; if th' other two be brained like us,
the state totters.

Stephano Drink, servant monster, when I bid thee:
thy eyes are almost set in thy head.

Trinculo Where should they be set else? He were   10
a brave monster indeed if they were set in his tail.

Stephano My man-monster hath drowned his
tongue in sack. For my part, the sea cannot drown
me. I swam, ere I could recover the shore, five-and-
thirty leagues off and on, by this light. Thou shalt be   15
my lieutenant, monster, or my standard.

Trinculo Your lieutenant, if you list; he's no
standard.

Stephano We'll not run, Monsieur Monster.

Trinculo Nor go neither; but you'll lie like dogs,   20
and yet say nothing neither.

Stephano Mooncalf, speak once in thy life, if thou
beest a good mooncalf.

Caliban How does thy honor? Let me lick thy
shoe.
I'll not serve him; he is not valiant.   25

NOTES

1. *butt is out:* barrel of wine is empty.

2. *bear up . . . 'em:* a sailor's variation of "drink up."

4. *the folly:* the freak, i.e., Caliban.

6. *be brained:* in two senses, (1) have brains like ours, (2) as we have been brained, beaten over the head (by the wine) as we have been. The second meaning is ironic, understood by the audience but not by Trinculo or his onstage listeners.

9. *almost set:* almost disappeared, as in a sunset. In the next line, Trinculo takes the word in the sense of "placed."

14. *recover:* reach.

five and thirty leagues: approximately 100 miles; clearly a drunken exaggeration.

16. *standard:* standard bearer, ensign; a military rank.

18. *no standard:* punning in two senses on Stephano's use of the word: (1) Caliban is anything but normal or standard, (2) Caliban can hardly stand because he is so drunk.

20. *go:* walk.

25. *him:* Trinculo.

Trinculo Thou liest, most ignorant monster: I am
  in case to justle a constable. Why, thou deboshed
  fish thou, was there ever man a coward that hath
  drunk so much sack as I today? Wilt thou tell
  a monstrous lie, being but half a fish and half a   30
  monster?

Caliban Lo, how he mocks me! Wilt thou let him, my lord?

Trinculo "Lord," quoth he? That a monster should
  be such a natural!   35

Caliban Lo, lo, again! Bite him to death, I prithee.

Stephano Trinculo, keep a good tongue in your
  head. If you prove a mutineer — the next tree! The
  poor monster's my subject, and he shall not suffer
  indignity.

Caliban I thank my noble lord. Wilt thou be
    pleased   40
  To hearken once again to the suit I made to thee?

Stephano Marry, will I. Kneel and repeat it; I
  will stand, and so shall Trinculo.

Enter ARIEL, *invisible.*

Caliban As I told thee before, I am subject to a
    tyrant,
  A sorcerer, that by his cunning hath   45
  Cheated me of the island.

Ariel   Thou liest.

Caliban Thou liest, thou jesting monkey thou!
  I would my valiant master would destroy thee. I do
    not lie.

Stephano Trinculo, if you trouble him any more   50
  in's tale, by this hand, I will supplant some of your
  teeth.

Trinculo Why, I said nothing.

Stephano Mum then, and no more. — Proceed.

Caliban I say by sorcery he got this isle;   55
  From me he got it. If thy greatness will
  Revenge it on him — for I know thou dar'st,
  But this thing dare not —

27. *in case to:* ready to.

    justle: jostle, interfere or fight with.

    deboshed: debauched, drunk.

35. *natural:* a fool; Trinculo means that although a monster is by definition unnatural, this one is a natural as well.

36. *again!:* i.e., he has mocked me again.

37. *good tongue:* watch your mouth (tongue), or else.

38. *the next tree:* i.e., will be used as a gallows to hang Trinculo for mutiny or treason.

51. *supplant:* displace or remove.

58. *this thing:* Trinculo.

Stephano That's most certain.

Caliban Thou shalt be lord of it, and I'll serve   60
thee.

Stephano How now shall this be compassed?
Canst thou bring me to the party?

Caliban Yea, yea, my lord! I'll yield him thee
asleep,
Where thou mayst knock a nail into his head.

Ariel Thou liest; thou canst not.   65

Caliban What a pied ninny's this! Thou scurvy
patch!
I do beseech thy greatness give him blows
And take his bottle from him. When that's gone,
He shall drink naught but brine, for I'll not show
him
Where the quick freshes are.   70

Stephano Trinculo, run into no further danger:
interrupt the monster one word further and, by this
hand, I'll turn my mercy out o' doors and make a
stockfish of thee.

Trinculo Why, what did I? I did nothing. I'll go   75
farther off.

Stephano Didst thou not say he lied?

Ariel Thou liest.

Stephano Do I so? Take thou that! [*Strikes* TRINCULO.]
As you like this, give me the lie another time.   80

Trinculo I did not give the lie. Out o' your wits,
and hearing too? A pox o' your bottle! This can
sack and drinking do. A murrain on your monster,
and the devil take your fingers!

Caliban Ha, ha, ha!   85

Stephano Now forward with your tale. — Prithee
stand further off.

Caliban Beat him enough. After a little time
I'll beat him too.

Stephano   Stand farther. — Come, proceed.

---

61.   *compassed:* achieved, brought about.

62.   *party:* person (the "tyrant" Caliban serves), i.e., Prospero.

66.   *pied ninny:* a fool; "pied" refers to the multi-colored jester's costume worn by Trinculo.

    patch: clown, from the patched dress.

69.   *brine:* salty sea water.

70.   *quick freshes:* fresh-water springs.

73.   *turn . . . doors:* kick you out; show no mercy.

74.   *stockfish:* dried cod, tenderized by beating.

80.   *give me the lie:* tell me I lie.

82.   *This:* This (threatening your friends with beatings) is the result of too much drink.

83.   *murrain:* plague, disease.

Caliban Why, as I told thee, 'tis a custom with him   90
I' th' afternoon to sleep: there thou mayst brain him,
Having first seized his books, or with a log
Batter his skull, or paunch him with a stake,
Or cut his wesand with thy knife. Remember
First to possess his books; for without them   95
He's but a sot, as I am, nor hath not
One spirit to command. They all do hate him
As rootedly as I. Burn but his books.
He has brave utensils (for so he calls them)
Which, when he has a house, he'll deck withal.   100
And that most deeply to consider is
The beauty of his daughter. He himself
Calls her a nonpariel. I never saw a woman
But only Sycorax my dam and she,
But she as far surpasseth Sycorax   105
As great'st does least.

Stephano   Is it so brave a lass?

Caliban Ay, lord. She will become thy bed, I
    warrant,
And bring thee forth brave brood.

Stephano Monster, I will kill this man: his daughter
and I will be king and queen, — save our Graces! —   110
and Trinculo and thyself shall be viceroys. Dost thou
like the plot, Trinculo?

Trinculo Excellent.

Stephano Give me thy hand. I am sorry I beat
thee; but while thou liv'st, keep a good tongue in thy   115
head.

Caliban Within this half hour will he be asleep.
Wilt thou destroy him then?

Stephano   Ay, on mine honor.

Ariel This will I tell my master.

Caliban Thou mak'st me merry; I am full of   120
    pleasure.
Let us be jocund. Will you troll the catch
You taught me but whilere?

93.	*paunch:* i.e., stab him in the belly (paunch).
94.	*wesand:* windpipe.
96.	*sot:* fool.
99.	*utensils:* fine things, either magical or household furniture.
103.	*nonpareil:* without equal.
104.	*dam:* mother.
106.	*brave:* beautiful, attractive.
107.	*become thy bed:* be the ideal mother of your children.
108.	*brood:* children.
111.	*viceroys:* deputies to the king.
121.	*jocund:* happy, merry.
	troll the catch: sing the song; a catch was a part-song for three or more voices, sung as a round.
122.	*whilere:* just a little while ago.

Stephano At thy request, monster, I will do reason, any
reason. — Come on, Trinculo, let us sing.

Sings.
> Flout 'em and scout 'em   125
> And scout 'em and flout 'em!
> Thought is free.

Caliban That's not the tune.

ARIEL *plays the tune on a tabor and pipe.*

Stephano What is this same?

Trinculo This is the tune of our catch, played by   130
the picture of Nobody.

Stephano If thou beest a man, show thyself in thy
likeness. If thou beest a devil, take't as thou list.

Trinculo O, forgive me my sins!

Stephano He that dies pays all debts. I defy thee.   135
Mercy upon us!

Caliban Art thou afeard?

Stephano No, monster, not I.

Caliban Be not afeard: the isle is full of noises,
Sounds and sweet airs that give delight and hurt not.   140
Sometimes a thousand twangling instruments
Will hum about mine ears; and sometimes voices
That, if I then had waked after long sleep,
Will make me sleep again; and then, in dreaming,
The clouds methought would open and show riches   145
Ready to drop upon me, that, when I waked,
I cried to dream again.

Stephano This will prove a brave kingdom to me,
where I shall have my music for nothing.

Caliban When Prospero is destroyed.   150

Stephano That shall be by and by: I remember
the story.

Trinculo The sound is going away: let's follow it,
and after do our work.

---

123. *reason:* anything within reason.

125. *flout:* disregard or scorn authority.

scout: make fools of.

SD. *tabor and pipe:* small drum worn at the side and played with one hand while the other hand fingers a wooden flute.

131. *picture of Nobody:* the reference is to drawings of a man, No-body, composed of head, arms, and legs.

133. *as thou list:* any way you like.

135. In this single line, Stephano moves from bravery grounded in faith to utter fear.

140. *airs:* songs.

151. *by and by:* soon.

Stephano Lead, monster; we'll follow. I would I
could see this taborer: he lays it on. Wilt come?

155

Trinculo I'll follow, Stephano. *Exeunt.*

156.   *taborer:* maker of music.

lays it on: plays well.

COMMENTARY

Caliban pursues his earlier suggestion that Stephano assert himself as the master of the island in this scene, which shows the comic characters a few stages further along in their drunken revelry from when last we saw them. In the comic subplot, then, Shakespeare presents a humorous version in miniature of elements present in the main plot, namely Antonio's overthrow of Prospero as detailed in the background story told by Prospero in Act I, Scene 2, and of the second generation version of a similar plot with Sebastian overthrowing his brother, Alonso.

Caliban is a surprisingly effective architect of revolution and shows yet another dimension of his language skills here as he works to persuade Stephano to undertake the murder and overthrow of Prospero. In this short comic scene, virtually all of the seven deadly sins are practiced by the mutineers (especially by Caliban) and/or used as inspiration for further misdeeds. Caliban expresses envy and covetousness of Prospero's power, along with greed, sloth, pride, anger, and ongoing lust for Miranda. Caliban is perhaps raised to a slightly more human level here (although a decidedly despicable humanity), while Trinculo and Stephano are increasingly exposed as among the worst examples of humanity for Caliban to study.

Stephano, primed by drink, is easily persuaded to undertake the murderous plot Caliban proposes and quickly adopts in his language the fantasy of power, referring to Caliban as his "lieutenant" and referring later in the scene to both Caliban and Trinculo as "viceroys," or royal deputies.

Ariel causes mischief in this scene that should remind many readers of the sort of tricks performed by Puck in *A Midsummer Night's Dream*. Here, Ariel

"What a pied ninny's this!" (III.2.62). Caliban, in calling Trinculo a "pied ninny," refers to Trinculo's motley or parti-colored costume, the traditional garb for Trinculo's profession as a court jester.
Pushkin Museum of Fine Arts, Moscow, Russia/SuperStock

uses ventriloquism to cause tension among the drunken, would-be revolutionaries.

Caliban's language has power and a highly visual quality as he describes several methods for doing away with Prospero, be it by cutting his throat, bashing in his skull, or running a stake into his stomach. Caliban has clearly considered this before; he is wary of Prospero's power. He knows Prospero's magical powers lay in his learning and is therefore certain to stress and restress the fact that, before Stephano can kill Prospero, he must possess Prospero's magic books. The ultimate selling-point Caliban provides Stephano for following through on the proposed murder is the reward of Miranda. In his desire to have Stephano kill Prospero and marry Miranda, Caliban is asking his new-found "god" and master to act out his own fantasies.

At the scene's end, Ariel provides music to guide the plotters off stage. Stephano and Trinculo are initially frightened by these fantastic noises, but Caliban, accustomed to the strange magic of the island, is calm and lyrical in his praise of the "Sounds and sweet airs that give delight and hurt not" (line136). After he is over his initial fear, Stephano likes the idea of this mysterious music, remarking that such a magical isle will prove a delightful kingdom.

"Ariel plays the tabor and pipe" (III.2 Stage Direction). The tabor is a drum carried on a shoulder strap and played with one hand; the pipe is a wooden flute-like instrument with stops that can be fingered, likewise, with one hand. Thus, the tabor and pipe go a long way toward providing a one-person band.
Stadel Art Institute, Frankfurt am Main/SuperStock

Act III, Scene 3

Weary and exhausted by their unsuccessful search for Ferdinand, the court party sits down to rest. A strange banquet magically appears before them, but when they go to eat, it disappears. A Harpy appears and accuses Alonso, Sebastian, and Antonio of sinfulness. Alonso, struck by the truth of this, is repentant; Sebastian and Antonio are angered and prepare for a fight.

ACT III, SCENE 3.
[Another part of the island.]

Enter ALONSO, SEBASTIAN, ANTONIO, GONZALO,
    ADRIAN, FRANCISCO, *and Others.*

Gonzalo By'r Lakin, I can go no further, sir:
My old bones ache: here's a maze trod indeed
Through forthrights and meanders. By your patience
I needs must rest me.

Alonso   Old lord, I cannot blame thee,
Who am myself attached with weariness   5
To th' dulling of my spirits. Sit down and rest.
Even here I will put off my hope, and keep it
No longer for my flatterer: he is drowned
Whom thus we stray to find; and the sea mocks
Our frustrate search on land. Well, let him go.   10

Antonio [*Aside to* SEBASTIAN] I am right glad that
    he's so out of hope.
Do not for one repulse forgo the purpose
That you resolved t' effect.

Sebastian   [*Aside to* ANTONIO] The next
    advantage
Will we take throughly.

Antonio [*Aside to* SEBASTIAN] Let it be tonight;
For, now they are oppressed with travel, they   15
Will not nor cannot use such vigilance
As when they are fresh.

Sebastian [*Aside to* ANTONIO] I say tonight. No more.

Solemn and strange music; and PROSPERO *on the top (invisi-
    ble). Enter several strange Shapes, bringing in a banquet; and
    dance about it with gentle actions of salutations and, inviting
    the King,* ETC. *to eat, they depart.*

NOTES

1.   *By'r Lakin:* by our Ladykin (a diminutive of the Virgin Mary).

3.   *forthrights and meanders:* straightforward and twisting paths.

5.   *attached:* seized (a legal pun).

6.   *dulling:* exhaustion.

7.   *he is drowned:* Ferdinand, Alonso's son.

8.   *hope . . . flatterer:* i.e., no longer will I let hope keep me from the truth, that Ferdinand is drowned.

12.   *for one repulse:* because of one setback (the waking of the King and Gonzalo at II.1.309).

14.   *throughly:* thoroughly.

SD.   *on the top:* this may refer to a stage level above the upper stage, where the musicians sometimes sat. However, if the banquet is brought on from the inner stage (as seems likely), Prospero may appear on the upper stage. He wears a "gown for to go invisible" (see I.2.SD).

Alonso What harmony is this? My good friends, hark!

Gonzalo Marvelous sweet music!

Alonso Give us kind keepers, heavens! What were   20
these?

Sebastian A living drollery. Now I will believe
That there are unicorns; that in Arabia
There is one tree, the phoenix' throne; one phoenix
At this hour reigning there.

Antonio   I'll believe both;
And what does else want credit, come to me,   25
And I'll be sworn 'tis true. Travelers ne'er did lie,
Though fools at home condemn 'em.

Gonzalo   If in Naples
I should report this now, would they believe me
If I should say I saw such islanders?
(For certes these are people of the island)   30
Who, though they are of monstrous shape, yet note,
Their manners are more gentle, kind, than of
Our human generation you shall find
Many, nay, almost any.

Prospero [*Aside*]   Honest lord,
Thou hast said well; for some of you there present   35
Are worse than devils.

Alonso   I cannot too much muse
Such shapes, such gesture, and such sound, expressing
Although they want the use of tongue — a kind
Of excellent dumb discourse.

Prospero [*Aside*]   Praise in departing.

Francisco They vanished strangely.   40

Sebastian No matter, since
They have left their viands behind; for we have
stomachs.
Will't please you taste of what is here?

Alonso   Not I.

20.	*keepers:* guardian spirits.
21.	*drollery:* a puppet show.
23.	*phoenix:* mythical bird from Arabian legend. Only one phoenix lives at any time, and every 100 years it explodes in fire and regenerates from its own ashes. A symbol of resurrection and rebirth.
25.	*what . . . credit:* anything else previously held to be unbelievable.
30.	*certes:* certainly.
32.	*gentle, kind:* well-behaved, elegant.
35.	*muse:* marvel or wonder at.
39.	*Praise in departing:* from the proverb, "Do not praise the host's meal until you have eaten it."
41.	*viands:* food.
	stomachs: appetites.

Gonzalo Faith, sir, you need not fear. When we
    were boys,
Who would believe that there were mountaineers
Dewlapped like bulls, whose throats had hanging
    at 'em   45
Wallets of flesh? or that there were such men
Whose heads stood in their breasts? which now we
    find
Each putter-out of five for one will bring us
Good warrant of.

Alonso   I will stand to, and feed;
Although my last, no matter, since I feel   50
The best is past. Brother, my lord the Duke,
Stand to, and do as we.

Thunder and lightning. Enter ARIEL *(like a harpy); claps his*
    wings upon the table; and with a quaint device the banquet
    vanishes.

Ariel You are three men of sin, whom destiny —
That hath to instrument this lower world
And what is in't — the never-surfeited sea   55
Hath caused to belch up you, and on this island,
Where man doth not inhabit, you 'mongst men
Being most unfit to live, I have made you mad;
And even with such-like valor men hang and drown
Their proper selves.   60

[ALONSO, SEBASTIAN, ANTONIO, ETC. *draw their*
    swords]
        You fools! I and my fellows
Are ministers of Fate. The elements,
Of whom your swords are tempered, may as well
Wound the loud winds, or with bemocked-at stabs
Kill the still-closing waters, as diminish
One dowle that's in my plume. My fellow ministers   65
Are like invulnerable. If you could hurt,
Your swords are now too massy for your strengths
And will not be uplifted. But remember
(For that's my business to you) that you three
From Milan did supplant good Prospero;   70
Exposed unto the sea, which hath requit it,
Him and his innocent child; for which foul deed

45. *Dewlapped:* folds of skin on a cow or bull.

47. *in their breasts:* a travelers' tale, also referred to in *Othello,* "... men whose heads / Do grow beneath their shoulders."

48. *Each putter-out ... one:* a voyager to the New World could deposit a sum in London, which was forfeit if he failed to return and repaid five-fold if he returned safely; an early form of travel insurance and speculation.

30. *harpy:* a mythical beast having the head of a woman and the body, wings, and talons of an eagle; supposed to act as an agent of vengeance.

quaint: ingenious, clever; the reference is to some sort of mechanical stage device.

53. *You:* Alonso, Antonio, and Sebastian.

destiny: i.e., destiny, which controls the earth and those in it, has caused the sea to spit you out on to this island.

59. *such-like valor:* bravery inspired by madness.

64. *still:* constantly.

65. *dowle:* small feather.

66. *like:* also, equally.

71. *requit it:* avenged betrayal of Prospero.

The powers, delaying, not forgetting, have
Incensed the seas and shores, yea, all the creatures,
Against your peace. Thee of thy son, Alonso,   75
They have bereft; and do pronounce by me
Ling'ring perdition (worse than any death
Can be at once) shall step by step attend
You and your ways; whose wraths to guard you from
Which here, in this most desolate isle, else falls   80
Upon your heads — is nothing but heart's sorrow
And a clear life ensuing.

*He vanishes in thunder; then (to soft music), enter the Shapes
again, and dance with mocks and mows, and carry out the
table.*

Prospero Bravely the figure of this harpy hast thou
Performed my Ariel; a grace it had devouring.
Of my instruction hast thou nothing bated   85
In what thou hadst to say. So, with good life
And observation strange, my meaner ministers
Their several kinds have done. My high charms work,
And these, mine enemies, are all knit up
In their distractions: they now are in my power;   90
And in these fits I leave them, while I visit
Young Ferdinand, whom they suppose is drowned,
And his and mine loved darling. [*Exit above.*]

Gonzalo I' th' name of something holy, sir, why
    stand you
In this strange stare?   95

Alonso   O, it is monstrous, monstrous!
Methought the billows spoke and told me of it;
The winds did sing it to me; and the thunder,
That deep and dreadful organ pipe, pronounced
The name of Prosper; it did bass my trespass.
Therefore my son i' th' ooze is bedded; and   100
I'll seek him deeper than e'er plummet sounded
And with him there lie mudded. *Exit.*

Sebastian   But one fiend at a time,
I'll fight their legions o'er!

Antonio   I'll be thy second.

[*Exeunt* SEBASTIAN *and* ANTONIO.]

76.	*bereft:* taken away.
77.	*lingering perdition:* a slow, painful death as punishment.
79 ff.	*guard . . . ensuing:* i.e., your only hope of avoiding a torturous death is to repent and immediately begin leading a life of decency and goodness.
SD.	*mocks and mows:* grimaces and gestures.
84.	*devouring:* i.e., making the banquet vanish.
85.	*bated:* omitted, forgotten.
87.	*observation strange:* unusual attention.
88.	*several kinds:* various tasks.
89.	*knit up:* bound up; entwined.
94.	*why . . . stare?:* i.e., why do you stare in wonder? (See Commentary.)
96.	*billows:* ocean waves.
99.	*bass my trespass:* provide a bass, musically, for the statement of his guilt. All of Nature is singing out in accusation.
103.	*o'er:* over: i.e., all of them.

Gonzalo All three of them are desperate: their
    great guilt,
Like poison given to work a great time after,   105
Now gins to bite the spirits. I do beseech you,
That are of suppler joints, follow them swiftly
And hinder them from what this ecstasy
May now provoke them to.

Adrian   Follow, I pray you.

Exeunt omnes

104.   *desperate:* reckless.

        their great guilt: Gonzalo assumes that self-knowl-
        edge of their guilt is now at work.

108.   *ecstasy:* madness.

COMMENTARY

Alonso and the court party continue to wander about the island as if in a maze, as Gonzalo notes. It is almost as if even Gonzalo is now willing to admit that the search for Ferdinand is a useless one. Alonso is certainly beyond all hope that his son has escaped drowning and is even more convinced of this than before. The entire party is weary, hungry, and thirsty.

When Ariel and the other spirit helpers appear ushering in the magical banquet — observed perhaps from the musicians' gallery above the stage by Prospero — the refreshment they offer is all the more appealing to these beleaguered men.

"Now I will believe . . . There is one tree, the phoenix's throne; one phoenix / At this hour reigning there" (III.3.21–23). Sebastian, amazed by the "strange shapes" who present the banquet before the travel-weary court party, proclaims his willingness to believe in such fantastic things as unicorns or the phoenix, a mythical Arabian bird said to be consumed once every thousand years in flame, only to be reborn from its own ashes.

The staging of this scene is highly elaborate and contains some of the most detailed stage directions written by Shakespeare (who wrote very few explicit stage directions). That Shakespeare did provide such detailed stage directions for the banquet and its disappearance "by a quaint device" (line 52), for the presentation of Ariel as a Harpy and in the next act for the wedding masque shows the play's affinity to the masques that were growing in popularity at James I's court and is again a reminder that the first two known performances of this play were staged before the King at his palace at Whitehall. These masques, as noted in the introduction, have far more to do with visual spectacle and music than regular plays. We can especially see the influence of the court masque in the enhanced attention to visual detail that Shakespeare affords this scene and the scene to follow.

It is unclear *how* exactly the banquet would have been presented, although the numerous references to elements of fantasy (unicorns, the mythical phoenix, the dew-lapped bullmen) suggest that it must have been an amazing spectacle. The thematic significance, however, is easier to decipher.

The banquet itself follows in reverse order of the traditional masque structure, moving here from beauty and order to darkness, disorder, and cacophony. Ariel prevents the court party from partaking of the tempting feast, appearing in the form of a Harpy, a mythological creature with the face of a woman and the body of an eagle. Ariel appears as a dangerous, threatening, and accusatory figure, who exposes Alonso, Antonio, and Sebastian as "three men of sin."

The banquet itself and the temptation it represents are precisely what Alonso, Antonio, and Sebastian have spent their lives pursuing: worldly material wealth and power. Prospero has brought them here to expose them for this sinfulness and to punish them for the lengths they have gone in striving to amass wealth and power. They immediately draw their swords in an effort to fight the spirit world with physical strength, only to be laughed at and made powerless by Ariel's magic. Their strength is taken away and their swords made too heavy for them to lift. The sins they committed against Prospero, in particular, have been neither forgotten nor forgiven. In partial repayment for these sins, Ariel announces, Ferdinand has died; this is only the beginning of the tortures or lingering perdition these three are to experience, *unless* they repent of their sins and resolve to lead a decent life hereafter.

Ariel vanishes in thunder, a thunder in which Alonso believes he hears Prospero's name as a reminder of his betrayal. In this way, Shakespeare's use of thunder as reminiscent of Prospero's name or voice recalls Caliban's fears at the opening of Act II, Scene 2, that Prospero would torment him with snakes, adders, cramps, and other physical tortures. Remember that Caliban reacts specifically to the noise of thunder as a sign that Prospero is displeased and is sending magical spirits to torture Caliban.

Gonzalo clearly sees the banquet, but it is unclear if he also sees Ariel in the figure of the Harpy or if that was a vision seen only by the three men of sin. Gonzalo's words at line 94 suggest that he did not see the horrific vision of accusation. Gonzalo understands from Alonso's comment that the thunder "did bass [his] trespass," or speak of his sins, and that guilt has finally caught up with Alonso, and possibly with Antonio as well. Clearly, it is passionate emotions that reinvigorate

"Who would believe . . . there were such men / Whose heads stood in their breasts?" (III.3.44–47). Gonzalo, like Sebastian, Antonio, and Alonso, is amazed by the strange creatures who present the banquet. Like Sebastian's reference to the phoenix, Gonzalo alludes to the tales often told by travelers, wherein reports of strange and mysterious creatures abounded. His description of "men / Whose heads stood in their breasts" sounds very much like the description Shakespeare's Othello gives to "The Anthropophagi and men whose heads / Do grow beneath their shoulders" (Othello, I.3.156–157).

Alonso, Antonio, and Sebastian, who are nearly exhausted with travel at the opening of this scene, to exit in a passion, with swords drawn (in the case of Antonio and Sebastian). Fearful for their safety, Gonzalo instructs the two young lords, Francisco and Adrian, to follow Alonso, Antonio, and Sebastian closely and protect them if they can.

The whole of this scene is a powerful echo of a similar episode in Book III of Virgil's epic the *Aeneid*, referenced before in Gonzalo's discussion of "Widow Dido." In the parallel episode from Virgil's epic — a standard grammar school text in Shakespeare's day — Aeneas and his men arrive on the island of the Harpies and are presented with a tempting but interrupted banquet, followed by a thunderous prophecy.

> Shaking out their wings with a great clanging, the Harpies, horrible, swoop from the hilltops; and plundering our banquet with the filthy touch of their talons, they foul everything. Their terrifying scream leaps from their stench.
> III.295–9

(Trans. Allen Mandelbaum, Bantam Classics, 1981)

Later in Virgil's story, the hero Aeneas visits the underworld and witnesses the tortures to which sinful men and women are subjected:

> . . . and there are those who sit before high banquet couches, gleaming upon supports of gold; before their eyes a feast is spread in royal luxury, but near at hand reclines the fiercest Fury:
> they cannot touch the tables lest she leap with lifted torch and thundering outcries.
> VI.603–8

These two passages almost certainly primed Shakespeare's imagination. As discussed in the Introduction, the study of Shakespeare's use of sources is interesting not merely as the process of identifying verbal echoes, but also in noting the source's influence on the larger shaping of the play and its thematic importance.

Notes

CLIFFSCOMPLETE

THE TEMPEST
ACT IV

Prospero *A devil, a born devil, on whose nature*
Nurture can never stick: on whom my pains,
Humanely taken, all, all lost, quite lost!
And as with age his body uglier grows,
So his mind cankers. I will plague them all,
Even to roaring.

Act IV, Scene 1

Prospero rewards Ferdinand's labors with the promise of marriage to Miranda but adds a stern warning that Ferdinand protect Miranda's virginity until a proper marriage takes place. Prospero commands Ariel to present a masque before the young lovers; the entertainment ends abruptly when Prospero suddenly remembers Caliban's murderous plot. Caliban brings Stephano and Trinculo to Prospero's cell, where they are distracted by fancy clothing and chased away by Prospero's hell hounds.

ACT IV, SCENE 1.
[Before Prospero's cell.]

Enter PROSPERO, FERDINAND, *and* MIRANDA.

Prospero If I have too austerely punished you,
Your compensation makes amends; for I
Have given you here a third of mine own life,
Or that for which I live; who once again
I tender to thy hand. All thy vexations   5
Were but my trials of thy love, and thou
Hast strangely stood the test. Here, afore heaven,
I ratify this my rich gift. O Ferdinand,
Do not smile at me that I boast her off,
For thou shalt find she will outstrip all praise   10
And make it halt behind her.

Ferdinand　　　　　　　　　　I do believe it
Against an oracle.

Prospero Then, as my gift, and thine own acquisi-
tion Worthily purchased, take my daughter. But
If thou dost break her virgin-knot before   15
All sanctimonious ceremonies may
With full and holy rite be minist'red,
No sweet aspersion shall the heavens let fall
To make this contract grow; but barren hate,
Sour-eyed disdain, and discord shall bestrew   20
The union of your bed with weeds so loathly
That you shall hate it both. Therefore take heed,
As Hymen's lamp shall light you.

Ferdinand　　　　　　　　　　　As I hope
For quiet days, fair issue, and long life,

NOTES

1.　*austerely:* harshly.

3.　*a third:* Scholars disagree on the meaning of this line. The most likely interpretations are that Prospero holds three things as his most prized possessions: Miranda, Milan, and his own life; or, Miranda, Milan, and his books.

5.　*tender:* offer.

7.　*strangely:* remarkably; in a special way.

9.　*boast her off:* boast of her.

10.　*outstrip:* exceed.

11.　*halt:* go slowly; limp.

12.　*Against an oracle:* even if an oracle from the gods proclaimed otherwise.

16.　*sanctimonious:* sacred.

18.　*aspersion:* a sprinkling of heavenly grace; a blessing.

23.　*Hymen's lamp:* Hymen, the Greek god of marriage, was usually represented as carrying a torch and a veil to guide the newlywed couple to their marriage bed.

24.　*fair issue:* beautiful children.

With such love as 'tis now, the murkiest den,   25
The most opportune place, the strong'st suggestion
Our worser genius can, shall never melt
Mine honor into lust, to take away
The edge of that day's celebration
When I shall think or Phoebus' steeds are foundered   30
Or Night kept chained below.

Prospero   Fairly spoke.
Sit then and talk with her; she is thine own.
What, Ariel! my industrious servant, Ariel!

Enter ARIEL.

Ariel What would my potent master? Here I am.

Prospero Thou and thy meaner fellows your last   35
    service
Did worthily perform; and I must use you
In such another trick. Go bring the rabble,
O'er whom I give thee pow'r, here to this place.
Incite them to quick motion; for I must
Bestow upon the eyes of this young couple   40
Some vanity of mine art: it is my promise,
And they expect it from me.

Ariel   Presently?

Prospero Ay, with a twink.

Ariel Before you can say "Come" and "Go,"
And breathe twice and cry, "So, so,"   45
Each one, tripping on his toe,
Will be here with mop and mow.
Do you love me, master? No?

Prospero Dearly, my delicate Ariel. Do not approach
Till thou dost hear me call.

Ariel   Well: I conceive. *Exit.*   50

Prospero Look thou be true: do not give dalliance
Too much the rein: the strongest oaths are straw
To th' fire i' th' blood. Be more abstemious,
Or else good night your vow!

---

25 ff. *With love . . . below:* Ferdinand claims that, while his love is pure and will not lead to lust, when the marriage day does arrive, he will barely be able to wait for the wedding night.

27. *worser genius:* bad spirit.

can: i.e., can make.

37. *rabble:* the rest of the spirits or "meaner fellows" at line 35.

41. *vanity:* display, show.

art: magic.

42. *Presently:* at once.

43. *with a twink:* in the blink of an eye.

47. *mop and mow:* facial gestures appropriate to entertain.

50. *conceive:* understand.

51 ff. *Look thou be true:* Prospero warns the couple not to be too familiar too soon.

52. *too much rein:* i.e., don't let your horses run uncontrolled; hold your horses.

53. *abstemious:* restrained, self-controlled.

Ferdinand   I warrant you, sir.
  The white cold virgin snow upon my heart   55
  Abates the ardor of my liver.

Prospero   Well.
  Now come, my Ariel: bring a corollary
  Rather than want a spirit. Appear, and pertly!
  No tongue! All eyes! Be silent.

Soft music

Enter IRIS.

Iris Ceres, most bounteous lady, thy rich leas   60
  Of wheat, rye, barley, vetches, oats, and pease;
  Thy turfy mountains, where live nibbling sheep,
  And flat meads thatched with stover, them to keep;
  Thy banks with pioned and twilled brims,
  Which spongy April at thy hest betrims   65
  To make cold nymphs chaste crowns; and thy broom groves,
  Whose shadow the dismissed bachelor loves,
  Being lasslorn; thy pole-clipt vineyard;
  And thy sea-marge, sterile and rocky-hard,
  Where thou thyself dost air — the queen o' th' sky,   70
  Whose wat'ry arch and messenger am I,
  Bids thee leave these, and with her sovereign grace,
  Here on this grass-plot, in this very place.
  To come and sport: her peacocks fly amain.
  Approach, rich Ceres, her to entertain.   75

Enter CERES.

Ceres Hail, many-colored messenger, that ne'er
  Dost disobey the wife of Jupiter,
  Who, with thy saffron wings, upon my flow'rs
  Diffusest honey drops, refreshing show'rs,
  And with each end of thy blue bow dost crown   80
  My bosky acres and my unshrubbed down,
  Rich scarf to my proud earth — why hath thy queen
  Summoned me hither to this short-grassed green?

Iris A contract of true love to celebrate
  And some donation freely to estate   85
  On the blessed lovers.

Ceres   Tell me, heavenly bow,
  If Venus or her son, as thou dost know,

56.	*liver:* the supposed seat of passion. Ferdinand protests that his chaste purity is stronger still than his amorous (lustful) desire.
57.	*corollary:* an extra.
58.	*want:* lack or need.
	pertly: swiftly.
SD.	*Iris:* the female messenger of the gods, and also the spirit of the rainbow.
60.	*Ceres:* goddess of the earth and patroness of agriculture.
61.	*vetches:* hay.
63.	*meads:* meadows or fields.
	stover: winter food for cattle.
64.	*pioned and twilled:* dug under by the current and protected against erosion by branches woven together (Arden edition, second series).
65.	*spongy:* damp, rainy.
	hest:: command.
66.	*broom groves:* coarse thickets.
68.	*lasslorn:* i.e., having lost his lass.
	pole-clipt: pruned.
70.	*queen o' th' sky:* Juno.
71.	*wat'ry arch:* rainbow.
74.	*peacocks:* birds usually associated with Juno, often pulling her chariot.
77.	*wife of Jupiter:* Juno.
78.	*saffron:* a multi-colored flower (white, purple, and yellow), and also a yellowish-orange used often in dyes.
79.	*Diffusest:* sprinkles.
81.	*bosky:* wooded, the opposite of "unshrubbed," later in the line.
85.	*estate:* give, make "in the state" of a gift.
87.	*Venus or her son:* Venus, the goddess of love, is mother to Cupid.

Do now attend the queen? Since they did plot
The means that dusky Dis my daughter got,
Her and her blind boy's scandalled company   90
I have forsworn.

Iris   Of her society
Be not afraid: I met her Diety
Cutting the clouds towards Paphos, and her son
Dove-drawn with her. Here thought they to have done
Some wanton charm upon this man and maid,   95
Whose vows are, that no bed-right shall be paid
Till Hymen's torch be lighted; but in vain.
Mars's hot minion is returned again;
Her waspish-headed son has broke his arrows,
Swears he will shoot no more, but play with sparrows 100
And be a boy right out.

Enter JUNO.

Ceres   Highest queen of state,
Great Juno, comes; I know her by her gait.

Juno How does my bounteous sister? Go with me
To bless this twain, that they may prosperous be
And honored in their issue.   105

They sing.

Juno Honor, riches, marriage blessing,
       Long continuance, and increasing,
       Hourly joys be still upon you!
       Juno sings her blessings on you.

Ceres Earth's increase, foison plenty,   110
       Barns and garners never empty,
       Vines with clust'ring bunches growing,
       Plants with goodly burden bowing;
       Spring come to you at the farthest
       In the very end of harvest.   115
       Scarcity and want shall shun you,
       Ceres' blessing so is on you.

Ferdinand This is a most majestic vision, and
Harmonious charmingly. May I be bold
To think these spirits?   120

89. *dusky:* dark, with reference to the underworld ruled by Dis.

my daughter got: Dis, or Pluto, kidnapped Prosperpine, Ceres' daughter, taking her to the underworld. Angered by this, Ceres cursed the world with winter.

90. *blind boy:* Cupid, usually pictured as blindfolded because "love is blind."

scandalled: scandalous; Cupid is associated with desire or lust.

92. *her Diety:* her divine majesty.

93. *Paphos:* the birthplace of Venus and the center of her cult.

94. *Dove-drawn:* Venus's chariot was usually represented as being drawn by doves.

95. *wanton charm:* a magic spell to incite lust.

97. *in vain:* i.e., Venus and Cupid have come in vain.

98. *Mars's hot minion:* Venus is the lover of Mars, the Greek god of war.

is returned again: has gone back.

99. *waspish:* able to sting (with his arrows).

101. *right out:* outright, completely.

102. *her gait:* her manner of moving which, as queen of the gods, is recognizably regal.

108. *still:* continually.

110. *foison:* abundance.

111. *garners:* granaries (grain silos).

114. *Spring come to you:* Ceres announces that spring will follow the harvest (autumn), thus there will be no winter; she repeals her curse for the abduction of Proserpine.

119. *charmingly:* magical.

Prospero   . Spirits, which by mine art
I have from their confines called to enact
My present fancies.

Ferdinand   Let me live here ever!
So rare a wond'red father and a wise
Makes this place Paradise.

JUNO *and* CERES *whisper, and send* IRIS *on employment.*

Prospero   Sweet now, silence!
Juno and Ceres whisper seriously.   125
There's something else to do. Hush and be mute,
Or else our spell is marred.

Iris You nymphs, call naiads, of the windring
          brooks,
With your sedged crowns and ever-harmless looks,
Leave your crisp channels, and on this green land   130
Answer your summons; Juno does command.
Come, temperate nymphs, and help to celebrate
A contract of true love: be not too late.

Enter certain Nymphs.
You sunburned sicklemen, of August weary,
Come hither from the furrow and be merry.   135
Make holiday: your rye-straw hats put on,
And these fresh nymphs encounter every one
In country footing.

*Enter certain Reapers, properly habited. They join with the
    Nymphs in a graceful dance; towards the end wherof PROS-
    PERO starts suddenly and speaks; after which, to a strange,
    hollow, and confused noise, they heavily vanish.*

Prospero [*Aside*] I had forgot that foul conspiracy
Of the beast Caliban and his confederates   140
Against my life: the minute of their plot
Is almost come. [*To the Spirits*] Well done! Avoid!
          No more!

Ferdinand This is strange. Your father's in some
          passion
That works him strongly.

Miranda   Never till this day
Saw I him touched with anger so distempered.   145

123.   *wond'red:* both to be wondered at and capable of producing wonders.

127.   *naiads:* water-nymphs.

       windring: a combination of winding and wandering.

129.   *sedged:* sedge is a water plant.

130.   *crisp:* rippled with small waves.

134.   *sicklemen:* farmers with sickles or scythes for cutting wheat.

       of August weary: worn out from their August work (reaping and harvesting).

135.   *furrow:* plowed field rows.

138.   *footing:* dancing.

SD.   *properly habited:* in appropiate costumes.

SD.   *heavily:* sadly, with regret and also clumsily.

141.   *minute:* the time appointed for.

142.   *Avoid!:* be gone.

144.   *works:* agitates, bothers.

145.   *distempered:* out of temper, harsh.

Prospero You do look, my son, in a moved sort,
  As if you were dismayed: be cheerful, sir.
  Our revels now are ended. These our actors,
  As I foretold you, were all spirits and
  Are melted into air, into thin air;   150
  And, like the baseless fabric of this vision,
  The cloud-capped towers, the gorgeous palaces,
  The solemn temples, the great globe itself,
  Yea, all which it inherit, shall dissolve,
  And, like this insubstantial pageant faded,   155
  Leave not a rack behind. We are such stuff
  As dreams are made on, and our little life
  Is rounded with a sleep. Sir, I am vexed.
  Bear with my weakness: my old brain is troubled.
  Be not disturbed with my infirmity.   160
  If you be pleased, retire into my cell
  And there repose. A turn or two I'll walk
  To still my beating mind.

Ferdinand, Miranda   We wish your peace. *Exeunt*
  [FERDINAND *and* MIRANDA].

Enter ARIEL.

Prospero Come with a thought! I thank thee,
  Ariel. Come.

Ariel Thy thoughts I cleave to. What's thy   165
  pleasure?

Prospero Spirit,
  We must prepare to meet with Caliban.

Ariel Ay, my commander: when I presented Ceres,
  I thought to have told thee of it, but I feared
  Lest I might anger thee.

Prospero Say again, where didst thou leave these   170
  varlets?

Ariel I told you, sir, they were red-hot with
  drinking:
  So full of valor that they smote the air
  For breathing in their faces, beat the ground
  For kissing of their feet; yet always bending
  Towards their project. Then I beat my tabor;   175
  At which like unbacked colts they pricked their ears,

---

146. *moved sort:* troubled state.

148. *revels:* the show Prospero created.

151. *baseless fabric:* spectacle without foundation; pure fancy.

154. *which it inherit:* who live there or possess it.

156. *rack:* wisp of cloud and also rack or frame of stage scenery.

157. *on:* of.

158. *rounded:* finished off, concluded.

    vexed: troubled.

162. *repose:* rest.

164. *I thank thee:* to Ferdinand and Miranda, for their wishes of peace.

167. *presented:* introduced in the masque, the director of a masque was sometimes called the "presenter"; possibly also suggesting that Ariel played the part of Ceres.

170. *varlets:* low-lifes.

176. *unbacked:* that had never been ridden; unbroken.

Advanced their eyelids, lifted up their noses
As they smelt music. So I charmed their ears
That calf-like they my lowing followed through
Toothed briers, sharp furzes, pricking goss, and thorns,   180
Which ent'red their frail shins. At last I left them
I' th' filthy mantled pool beyond your cell,
There dancing tip to th' chins, that the foul lake
O'erstunk their feet.

Prospero   This was well done, my bird.
Thy shape invisible retain thou still.   185
The trumpery in my house, go bring it hither
For stale to catch these thieves.

Ariel   I go, I go. *Exeunt.*

Prospero A devil, a born devil, on whose nature
Nurture can never stick: on whom my pains,
Humanely taken, all, all lost, quite lost!   190
And as with age his body uglier grows,
So his mind cankers. I will plague them all,
Even to roaring.

Enter ARIEL, *loaden with glistering apparel, etc.*
                    Come, hang them on this line.

[PROSPERO *and* ARIEL, *remain, invisible.*]

Enter CALIBAN, STEPHANO *and* TRINCULO, *all wet.*

Caliban Pray you tread softly, that the blind mole
    may not
Hear a foot fall. We now are near his cell.   195

Stephano Monster, your fairy, which you say is a
    harmless fairy, has done little better than played the
    Jack with us.

Trinculo Monster, I do smell all horse-piss, at
    which my nose is in great indignation.   200

Stephano So is mine. Do you hear, monster? If
    I should take a displeasure against you, look you, —

Trinculo Thou wert but a lost monster.

Caliban Good my lord, give me thy favor still.
    Be patient, for the prize I'll bring thee to   205

---

177.   *Advanced:* raised.

178.   *As:* as if.

180.   *goss:* gorse (prickly hedges).

182.   *filthy mantled:* covered with scum; Prospero's cistern or septic tank.

184.   *o'erstunk their feet:* covered them over with foul smells.

186.   *trumpery:* the "glistering apparel" of the stage direction below.

187.   *stale:* a stuffed bird used as a decoy; here, simply a decoy or bait.

188–189.   *nature . . . Nurture:* here "nature" represents uncivilized, animal being, while "nurture" is education and civilization in the broadest sense.

192.   *cankers:* rots from within.

193.   *line:* probably a lime tree.

195.   *Hear:* moles, because blind, were believed to have extra-sensitive hearing.

198.   *the Jack:* the knave (as in a deck of cards); also in the sense of jack o' lantern or will o' the wisp, which misled travelers (see note in Act II, Scene 2).

203.   *wert:* will be.

Shall hoodwink this mischance. Therefore speak
  softly.
All's hushed as midnight yet.

Trinculo Ay, but to lose our bottles in the pool, —

Stephano There is not only disgrace and dishonor
in that, monster, but an infinite loss.   210

Trinculo That's more to me than my wetting. Yet
this is your harmless fairy, monster.

Stephano I will fetch off my bottle, though I be
o'er ears for my labor.

Caliban Prithee, my king, be quiet. Seest thou   215
  here?
This is the mouth o' th' cell. No noise, and enter.
Do that good mischief which may make this island
Thine own for ever, and I, thy Caliban,
For aye thy foot-licker.

Stephano Give me thy hand. I do begin to have   220
bloody thoughts.

Trinculo O King Stephano! O peer! O worthy
  Stephano, look what a wardrobe here is for thee!

Caliban Let it alone, thou fool! It is but trash.

Trinculo O, ho, monster! we know what belongs   225
to a frippery. O King Stephano!

Stephano Put off that gown, Trinculo, by this
hand, I'll have that gown!

Trinculo Thy Grace shall have it.

Caliban The dropsy drown this fool! What do you   230
  mean
To dote thus on such luggage? Let 't alone,
And do the murder first. If he awake,
From toe to crown he'll fill our skins with pinches,
Make us strange stuff.

Stephano Be you quiet, monster. Mistress line, is   235
not this my jerkin? [*Takes it down.*] Now is the
jerkin under the line. Now, jerkin, you are like to
lose your hair and prove a bald jerkin.

---

206. *hoodwink this mischance:* close your eyes to (i.e., forget) this accident.

213. *fetch off:* retrieve, get back.
o'er ears: i.e., underwater.

219. *for aye:* forever.

222. *O King Stephano!:* Trinculo discovers the "glistering apparel."

226. *frippery:* second-hand clothes shop.

230. *dropsy:* a disease that causes accumulation of fluid; here, meaning a general sense of accumulation or greed with a doubleplay on excessive drunkenness.

231. *luggage:* junk.

236. *jerkin:* a vest or waistcoat.

238. *lose your hair:* An old sailor's joke; the jerkin is "under the line," i.e., has crossed the equator, or equinoctial line. It was a tradition to shave the heads of sailors crossing the line for the first time.

Trinculo Do, do! We steal by line and level, an't
like your Grace.   240

Stephano I thank thee for that jest. Here's a garment
for't. Wit shall not go unrewarded while I am
king of this country. "Steal by line and level" is an
excellent pass of pate. There's another garment for't.

Trinculo Monster, come put some lime upon your   245
fingers, and away with the rest.

Caliban I will have none on't. We shall lose our time
And all be turned to barnacles, or to apes
With foreheads villainous low.

Stephano Monster, lay-to your fingers: help to   250
bear this away where my hogshead of wine is, or I'll
turn you out of my kingdom. Go to, carry this.

Trinculo And this.

Stephano Ay, and this.

*A noise of hunters heard. Enter diverse Spirits in shape of dogs
and hounds, hunting them about; PROSPERO and ARIEL
setting them on.*

Prospero Hey, Mountain, hey!   255

Ariel Silver! there it goes, Silver!

Prospero Fury, Fury! There, Tyrant, there! Hark.
hark!

[CALIBAN, STEPHANO, *and* TRINCULO *are driven out.*]
Go, charge my goblins that they grind their joints
With dry convulsions, shorten up their sinews
With aged cramps, and more pinch-spotted make   260
them
Than pard or cat o' mountain.

Ariel   Hark, they roar!

Prospero Let them be hunted soundly. At this hour
Lie at my mercy all mine enemies.
Shortly shall all my labors end, and thou
Shalt have the air at freedom. For a little,   265
Follow, and do me service. *Exeunt*

239. *line and level:* i.e., according to a carpenter's rule and level, accurately or properly.

244. *pass of pate:* effort of wit ("pate" meaning "head").

245. *lime:* birdlime, which was sticky; i.e., get to work and help us.

248. *barnacles:* probably meaning the barnacle goose rather than the shellfish, but either is plausible.

250. *lay-to:* use.

251. *hogshead:* barrel.

SD *dogs and hounds:* the hounds of hell.

255–256. *Mountain . . . Silver:* the names of the dogs.

258. *my goblins:* Stephano, Trinculo, and Caliban, because, like goblins, they work mischief.

259. *dry convulsions:* spasms

260. *aged:* of old age.

261. *pard or cat o' mountain:* leopard.

COMMENTARY

The play's likeness to the court masques comes fully into recognition in this scene when Prospero presents what is in essence a masque in celebration of marriage as a reward for Miranda and Ferdinand. The bulk of Ferdinand's trial is over, his hard labor certainly is finished, and he is here rewarded with Prospero's most prized possession, the "rich gift" of his daughter. Until the couple can be brought properly to church for a fully sanctioned and legal marriage ceremony, however, they are sternly reminded by Prospero to maintain their purity and chastity. Ferdinand should by now be seen as the complete opposite of Caliban. This does not mean that in a realistic sense Ferdinand does not still represent a sexual threat to Miranda should he decide to "love her and leave her." Prospero — if not Miranda — is aware of this threat, even though it seems altogether unlikely that Ferdinand would prove that vile of a character.

Prospero again calls on Ariel to present the magic. Ariel, moved by the kindness Prospero clearly displays for Miranda and Ferdinand, asks an interesting question: "Do you love me Master, no?" (line 48). Prospero dismisses the question, being too focused on the business at hand. These few lines say a great deal, however, about the dynamics of the parent-like relationship Prospero has with Ariel.

The masque that Prospero devises, like the court masques performed before King James I, draws heavily on classical mythology and relies significantly on scene, spectacle, and music. The show presents in miniature three of the thematic movements of the play writ large: the calm that emerges from the storm, the nobility of character that comes from extending forgiveness and grace, and the power of regeneration in nature.

"Ceres, most bounteous lady . . ." (IV.1.60). Ceres, one of the goddesses who appears in the wedding masque of Act IV, Scene 1, is the Roman goddess of the harvest. She is summoned in Prospero's masque by Iris, the messenger of the gods. Together, Iris and Ceres join Juno, queen of the gods, in celebrating the "contract of true love" (84) between Ferdinand and Miranda.

The first figure to appear is Iris, the messenger of the gods who appears most often in non-human form as a rainbow. Here, her gown is of a rainbow of colors. In Biblical imagery the rainbow is the symbol of God's promise that, after the time of Noah, He will no longer visit the earth with the worldwide destructiveness of flood. Similarly, in Greek and Roman mythology, the rainbow represents the promise of the calm after a storm. Iris calls on Ceres, goddess of the harvest, to join her in attending on Juno, queen of the gods.

Ceres, as a harvest goddess, is symbolic of fertility and regeneration. Regeneration and wealth in harvest are not guaranteed; Ceres bestows them on the worthy as reward and, as the myth maintains, causes the earth to die in winter as revenge for the abduction to the underworld of her daughter, Proserpine.

Juno, who appears as the moon and is associated with the protection of women, invites her "bounteous sister," Ceres, to join her in blessing Ferdinand and Miranda and bring health and joy to their marriage. Ceres agrees and in song announces that spring will follow harvest (winter will be passed over).

"Earth's increase, foison plenty, / Barns and garners never empty, / Vines and clustering bunches growing, / Plants with goodly burthen bowing; / Spring come to you at the farthest / In the very end of the harvest!" (IV.1.110–115). The wedding masque in Act IV, Scene 1, symbolizes the union of harvest and spring (winter is skipped over). The language throughout the masque, as these lines illustrate, invokes images of plenty and fertility.
Musee de Louvre, Paris/SuperStock

goddesses' significance as icons or symbols. Autumn and Spring are here seen coming together in a sort of marriage rite. Winter — or death — is passed over, and the movement is from the abundance of harvest to the immediate re-flowering of spring.

The dance and the music end abruptly and clumsily — they "heavily vanish," according to the stage direction. The masque, which is a pure product of Prospero's imagination, comes crashing to an end, because Prospero, having temporarily forgotten about the conspiracy of Caliban, Stephano, and Trinculo, suddenly remembers it.

The verse throughout the masque may seem awkward or lacking in some of the power that Shakespeare is able to command in writing. In part, this is a product of the form; the masque relied heavily on song, dance, and spectacle. The limited range of the verse here may well be a result of Shakespeare needing to conform the words to certain musical formulas and to the demands of visual spectacle.

The songs of the goddesses are followed by a dance by nymphs and reapers. The reapers indicate Autumn or harvest, as they are the men who cut down the full-grown wheat and bring it home as harvest. They then dance with the spring-like water nymphs, or naiads. In this way, the visual aspect of the dancers reinforces the words spoken by the goddesses as well as the

Ferdinand and Miranda notice that Prospero's recollection puts him into a foul mood. Prospero's explanation for the masque's abrupt ending is one of Shakespeare's most beautiful comments on the temporary nature of both dramatic art and life. "We are such stuff / As dreams are made on" (line 156–157), Prospero muses. His speech is filled with the sort of descriptions that present the similarities between life and theatre that fascinated Shakespeare throughout his career. When Prospero refers, for example, to "the great globe itself" at line 153, Shakespeare plays on the double meaning of not only the earth, which when considered in the infinity of God's time is merely a temporary thing (as ancient and eternal as it may seem to us humans), but also to the name of the playhouse jointly owned by himself and his fellow sharers in the King's Men. The

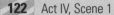
compact power of this movement in writing between transitory or temporary and permanent or eternal things is astounding and a mark of Shakespeare's full command of the manipulation of words and ideas at the pinnacle of his writing career.

Ariel reminds Prospero of the last known whereabouts of Caliban and his confederates. Having led them by music on a path as wandering and maze-like as that of which Gonzalo complained in Act III, Scene 1, Ariel then draws them into a stinking swamp or cesspool.

The next stage in Caliban, Stephano, and Trinculo's torment is a comically reduced version of the tempting banquet presented to Antonio, Alonso, and Stephano. Instead of a banquet, Ariel and Prospero leave out rich garments to tempt the lower-class desires of Stephano and Trinculo.

Caliban recognizes the costumes as worthless, a further distraction to prevent them from enacting their murderous rebellion. The conflicting desires of

"You sunburn'd sicklemen of August weary, / Come hither from the furrow and be merry" (IV.1.134–135). The masque concludes with a dance of reapers — "sunburn'd sicklemen" who have come from the work of harvesting grain — and the spring-like water nymphs of naiads.

the drunken conspirators cause them to fight and disagree, thus further decreasing the likelihood of their success.

The sounds of dogs or hellhounds frighten all three of the conspirators with the sorts of torments and tortures Caliban complains of earlier in the play. We should not forget Prospero's power, his anger, and his vindictiveness. At this point in the play, he is fully in control and has all his enemies entirely under his magical spell. The time for his revenge, as the play heads into its fifth and final act, has arrived: "At this hour / Lie at my mercy all mine enemies" (lines 262–263). The play holds some dramatic tension here as the audience wonders whether Prospero's anger and desire for revenge or his potential for kindness and desire to both extend and receive forgiveness will triumph in the final act. Will the fifth act cause this play to be a revenge tragedy, ending in blood, or a romantic comedy, ending (as romantic comedies by Shakespeare always end) in resolution and anticipation of marriage?

Notes

Notes

CLIFFSCOMPLETE

THE TEMPEST
ACT V

Ariel *His tears run down his beard like winter's drops*
From eaves of reeds. Your charm so strongly works 'em,
That if you now beheld them, your affections
Would become tender.

Act V, Scene 1

With all his enemies now in his power, Prospero must decide whether he will destroy them or forgive them. Ariel's description of the courtiers, especially Gonzalo, leads Prospero to pity. He resolves to forgive all and set Ariel free. Prospero removes Alonso's sadness for the son he supposes drowned, by revealing Ferdinand playing chess with Miranda. The sailors, as well as Stephano, Trinculo, and Caliban, are all brought onstage by Ariel: reunited, and found to be safe and alive. Happy plans are made for a return to Italy. All exit, leaving Prospero alone to speak an Epilogue to the audience.

ACT V, SCENE 1.
[Before Prospero's cell.]

Enter PROSPERO, *in his magic robes, and* ARIEL.

Prospero Now does my project gather to a head.
My charms crack not, my spirits obey, and time
Goes upright with his carriage. How's the day?

Ariel On the sixth hour, at which time, my lord,
You said our work should cease.   5

Prospero   I did say so
When first I raised the tempest. Say, my spirit,
How fares the King and 's followers?

Ariel   Confined together
In the same fashion as you gave in charge,
Just as you left them — all prisoners, sir,
In the line grove which weather-fends your cell.   10
They cannot budge till your release. The King,
His brother, and yours abide all three distracted,
And the remainder mourning over them,
Brimful of sorrow and dismay; but chiefly
Him that you termed, sir, the good old Lord Gonzalo.   15
His tears run down his beard like winter's drops
From eaves of reeds. Your charm so strongly works 'em,
That if you now beheld them, your affections
Would become tender.

Prospero   Dost thou think so, spirit?

Ariel Mine would, sir, were I human.   20

NOTES

1. Prospero's speech here has several references to *alchemy*, the Renaissance pseudoscience that aimed to turn base metals like lead and iron into gold.

   project: experiment.

   gather to a head: bring to a boil.

2. *My charms crack not :* i.e., my magic will not fail.

2–3. *time . . . carriage:* time's burden is light; i.e., there is little time left.

8. *gave in charge:* commanded, charged to be done.

10. *line grove:* a grove of lime trees.

   weather-fends: defends or protects from the weather.

17. *eaves of reeds:* i.e., a thatched roof.

18. *affections:* feelings, emotions.

Prospero   And mine shall.
Hast thou, which art but air, a touch, a feeling
Of their afflictions, and shall not myself,
One of their kind, that relish all as sharply
Passion as they, be kindlier moved than thou art?
Though with their high wrongs I am struck to th'   25
    quick,
Yet with my nobler reason 'gainst my fury
Do I take part. The rarer action is
In virtue than in vengeance. They being penitent,
The sole drift of my purpose doth extend
Not a frown further. Go, release them, Ariel.   30
My charms I'll break, their senses I'll restore,
And they shall be themselves.

Ariel   I'll fetch them, sir. [*Exit.*]

Prospero Ye elves of hills, brooks, standing lakes,
    and groves,
And ye that on the sands with printless foot
Do chase the ebbing Neptune, and do fly him   35
When he comes back; you demi-puppets that
By moonshine do the green sour ringlets make,
Whereof the ewe not bites; and you whose pastime
Is to make midnight mushrumps, that rejoice
To hear the solemn curfew; by whose aid   40
(Weak masters though ye be) I have bedimmed
The noontide sun, called forth the mutinous winds,
And 'twixt the green sea and the azured vault
Set roaring war; to the dread rattling thunder
Have I given fire and rifted Jove's stout oak   45
With his own bolt; the strong-based promontory
Have I made shake and by the spurs plucked up
The pine and cedar; graves at my command
Have waked their sleepers, oped, and let 'em forth
By my so potent art. But this rough magic   50
I here abjure; and when I have required
Some heavenly music (which even now I do)
To work mine end upon their senses that
This airy charm is for, I'll break my staff,
Bury it certain fathoms in the earth,   55
And deeper than did ever plummet sound
I'll drown my book.

---

23.   *relish:* feel.

24.   *kindlier:* used frequently by Shakespeare in a double sense, (1) more sympathetic, (2) more in accordance with my kind, which is human.

27.   *rarer:* both less frequent and nobler.

28.   *penitent:* remorseful and desiring forgiveness.

34.   *printless:* leaving no footprint (on the wet sand).

35.   *Neptune:* god of the sea and, as here, simply another word for "ocean."

     fly: flee from.

37.   *green sour ringlets:* fairy rings formed by toadstools.

39.   *mushrumps:* mushrooms.

43.   *azured vault:* blue sky.

45.   *rifted:* made a rift in, split.

46.   *bolt:* thunderbolt.

47.   *spurs:* roots.

49.   *oped:* opened.

52.   *heavenly music:* a reference to the Renaissance belief that divine music, known as the music of the spheres, held in order the universe and determined the motion of the planets.

53.   *their senses that:* the senses of those whom.

Solemn music.

Here enters ARIEL *before; then* ALONSO, *with a frantic ges-*
ture, attended by GONZALO; SEBASTIAN *and* ANTO-
NIO *in like manner, attended by* ADRIAN *and*
FRANCISCO. *They all enter the circle which* PROSPERO
had made, and there stand charmed; which PROSPERO
observing, speaks.

A solemn air, and the best comforter
To an unsettled fancy, cure thy brains,
Now useless, boiled within thy skull! There stand,   60
For you are spell-stopped.
Holy Gonzalo, honorable man,
Mine eyes, ev'n sociable to the show of thine,
Fall fellowly drops. The charm dissolves apace;
And as the morning steals upon the night,   65
Melting the darkness, so their rising senses
Begin to chase the ignorant fumes that mantle
Their clearer reason. O good Gonzalo,
My true preserver, and a loyal Sir
To him thou follow'st, I will pay thy graces   70
Home both in word and deed. Most cruelly
Didst thou, Alonso, use me and my daughter.
Thy brother was a furtherer in the act.
Thou art pinched for't now, Sebastian. Flesh and
      blood,
You, brother mine, that entertained ambition,   75
Expelled remorse and nature; who, with Sebastian
(Whose inward pinches therefore are most strong),
Would here have killed your king. I do forgive thee,
Unnatural though thou art. Their understanding
Begins to swell, and the approaching tide   80
Will shortly fill the reasonable shore,
That now lies foul and muddy. Not one of them
That yet looks on me or would know me. Ariel,
Fetch me the hat and rapier in my cell.
I will discase me, and myself present   85
As I was sometime Milan. Quickly, spirit!
Thou shalt ere long be free.

[Exit ARIEL, *and returns immediately.*]

Ariel [*sings and helps to attire him.*]
      Where the bee sucks, there suck I;

58.	*air:* song, music.
59.	*cure thy brains:* heal you from the madness I have put upon you
63.	*sociable to . . . thine:* sympathetic to the sight of yours.
64.	*Fall:* let fall.
	apace: quickly.
67.	*mantle:* cover, conceal.
70.	*graces:* both virtues and kind acts done for me.
71.	*Home:* to the utmost.
74.	*pinched:* caught and punished.
76.	*remorse:* pity.
	nature: i.e., the natural feeling for a brother.
79–80.	*understanding . . . swell:* i.e., they are coming out of their trance.
81.	*reasonable shore:* the shore of reason; the mind. Prospero uses the ocean's swelling tides as metaphor for learning as the process of swelling or growing understanding.
84.	*rapier:* sword; together with a hat, an essential part of a seventeenth-century gentleman's dress.
85.	*discase:* take off his magic robe.
86.	*sometime Milan:* i.e., when I was Duke of Milan.
SD.	Ariel sings of his expeinces as a fairy-like creature. The practical purpose of the song is to provide time for Prospero's costume change.

In a cowslip's bell I lie;
There I couch when owls do cry.   90
On the bat's back I do fly
After summer merrily.
Merrily, merrily shall I live now
Under the blossom that hangs on the bough.

Prospero Why, that's my dainty Ariel! I shall miss   95
  thee,
But yet thou shalt have freedom; so, so, so.
To the King's ship, invisible as thou art!
There shalt thou find the mariners asleep
Under the hatches. The master and the boatswain
Being awake, enforce them to this place,   100
And presently, I prithee.
Ariel. I drink the air before me, and return
Or ere your pulse twice beat. *Exit.*

Gonzalo All torment, trouble, wonder, and amazement
Inhabits here. Some heavenly power guide us   105
Out of this fearful country!

Prospero Behold, sir King,
The wronged Duke of Milan, Prospero.
For more assurance that a living prince
Does now speak to thee, I embrace thy body,
And to thee and thy company I bid   110
A hearty welcome.

Alonso   Whe'r thou be'st he or no,
Or some enchanted trifle to abuse me,
As late I have been, I not know. Thy pulse
Beats, as of flesh and blood; and, since I saw thee,
Th' affliction of my mind amends, with which,   115
I fear, a madness held me. This must crave
(An if this be at all) a most strange story.
Thy dukedom I resign and do entreat
Thou pardon me my wrongs. But how should
  Prospero
Be living and be here?   120

Prospero   First, noble friend,
Let me embrace thine age, whose honor cannot
Be measured or confined.

101.	*presently:* immediately.
102.	*drink the air:* devour the space.
103.	*or ere:* before.
106.	*fearful:* terrifyng.
111.	*Whe'r:* whether.
112.	*enchanted trifle:* magic trick.
	abuse: both deceive and harm.
115.	*amends:* mends, improves.
117.	*An if this be:* if this is really true.
118.	*entreat:* beg

Gonzalo   Whether this be
Or be not, I'll not swear.

Prospero   You do yet taste
Some subtleties o' th' isle, that will not let you
Believe things certain. Welcome, my friends all.   125
[*Aside to* SEBASTIAN *and* ANTONIO] But you, my
brace of lords, were I so minded,
I here could pluck his Highness' frown upon you,
And justify you traitors. At this time
I will tell no tales.

Sebastian [*Aside*]   The devil speaks in him.

Prospero No.
For you, most wicked sir, whom to call brother   130
Would even infect my mouth, I do forgive
The rankest fault — all of them; and require
My dukedom of thee, which perforce I know
Thou must restore.

Alonso   If thou beest Prospero,
Give us particulars of thy preservation;   135
How thou hast met us here, who three hours since
Were wracked upon this shore; where I have lost
(How sharp the point of this remembrance is!)
My dear son Ferdinand.

Prospero   I am woe for't, sir.

Alonso Irreparable is the loss, and patience   140
Says it is past her cure.

Prospero   I rather think
You have not sought her help, of whose soft grace
For the like loss I have her sovereign aid
And rest myself content.

Alonso   You the like loss?

Prospero As great to me as late; and, supportable   145
To make the dear loss, have I means much weaker
Than you may call to comfort you; for I
Have lost my daughter.

Alonso   A daughter?
O heavens, that they were living both in Naples,
The King and Queen there! That they were, I wish   150

123.	*yet:* still.
124.	*subtleties:* both deceptions and also special cooked confections or sweets made especially for elaborate banquets.
127.	*pluck:* pull down.
128.	*justify:* justly prove.
133.	*rankest:* worst.
	require: both request and demand.
134.	*perforce:* out of necessity; because you must.
139.	*woe for't:* sorry for it.
140.	*Irreparable:* beyond repair.
142.	*soft grace:* merciful comfort.
145.	*late:* recent.
146.	*dear:* grievous.

Myself were mudded in the oozy bed
Where my son lies. When did you lose your daughter?

Prospero In this last tempest. I perceive these lords
At this encounter do so much admire
That they devour their reason and scarce think   155
Their eyes do offices of truth, their words
Are natural breath. But, howsoev'r you have
Been justled from your senses, know for certain
That I am Prospero, and that very duke
Which was thrust forth of Milan, who most strangely   160
Upon this shore, where you were wracked, was
     landed
To be the lord on't. No more yet of this;
For 'tis a chronicle of day by day,
Not a relation for a breakfast, nor
Befitting this first meeting. Welcome, sir;   165
This cell's my court. Here have I few attendants,
And subjects none abroad. Pray you look in.
My dukedom since you have given me again,
I will requite you with as good a thing,
At least bring forth a wonder to content ye   170
As much as me my dukedom.

Here PROSPERO *discovers* FERDINAND *and* MIRANDA
     playing at chess.

Miranda Sweet lord, you play me false.

Ferdinand   No, my dearest love.
I would not for the world.

Miranda Yes, for a score of kingdoms you should
     wrangle,
And I would call it fair play.   175

Alonso   If this prove
A vision of the island, one dear son
Shall I twice lose.

Sebastian   A most high miracle!

Ferdinand Though the seas threaten, they are merciful.
I have cursed them without cause. [*Kneels.*]

Alonso   Now all the blessings
Of a glad father compass thee about!   180

---

151. *mudded . . . bed:* lying in the same muddy seabed.

154. *so much admire:* are so amazed.

156. *do offices of truth:* tell them the truth.

157. *natural breath:* i.e., silence.

158. *justled from:* jostled, or forced out of.

163. *chronicle of . . . day:* a story of boring, everyday things.

167. *abroad:* elsewhere.

170. *a wonder:* another play on Miranda's name.

SD. *discovers:* reveals, by pulling aside the curtain of the inner stage.

172. *play me false:* cheat.

174. *Yes, for . . . play:* i.e., Ferdinand may do what he likes to win, but Miranda will still consider it fair play.

176. *vision:* another illusion.

Arise, and say how thou cam'st here.

Miranda   O, wonder!
How many goodly creatures are there here!
How beauteous mankind is! O brave new world
That has such people in't!

Prospero   'Tis new to thee.

Alonso What is this maid with whom thou wast   185
    at play?
Your eld'st acquaintance cannot be three hours.
Is she the goddess that hath severed us
And brought us thus together?

Ferdinand   Sir, she is mortal;
But by immortal providence she's mine.
I chose her when I could not ask my father   190
For his advice, nor thought I had one. She
Is daughter to this famous Duke of Milan,
Of whom so often I have heard renown
But never saw before; of whom I have
Received a second life; and second father   195
This lady makes him to me.

Alonso   I am hers.
But, O, how oddly will it sound that I
Must ask my child forgiveness!

Prospero   There, sir, stop.
Let us not burden our remembrance with
A heaviness that's gone.   200

Gonzalo   I have inly wept,
Or should have spoke ere this. Look down, you gods,
And on this couple drop a blessed crown!
For it is you that have chalked forth the way
Which brought us hither.

Alonso   I say amen, Gonzalo.

Gonzalo Was Milan thrust from Milan that his   205
    issue
Should become kings of Naples? O, rejoice
Beyond a common joy, and set it down
With gold on lasting pillars: in one voyage
Did Claribel her husband find at Tunis

186.   *eld'st:* longest.

196.   *I am hers:* i.e., I am also her father (by marriage).

200.   *I . . . this:* I have been crying my own tears of joy, otherwise I would have spoken sooner.

203.   *chalked forth:* marked out the direction with chalk.

205.   *Milan . . . Milan:* (1) the Duke, (2) the city or dukedom.

208.   *lasting pillars:* permanent monuments.

And Ferdinand her brother found a wife   210
Where he himself was lost; Prospero his dukedom
In a poor isle; and all of us ourselves
When no man was his own.

Alonso   [*To* FERDINAND *and* MIRANDA] Give me
    your hands.
Let grief and sorrow still embrace his heart
That doth not wish you joy.   215

Gonzalo   Be it so! Amen!

Enter ARIEL, *with the* MASTER *and* BOATSWAIN
    amazedly following.
O, look, sir; look, sir! Here is more of us!
I prophesied, if a gallows were on land,
This fellow could not drown. Now, blasphemy,
That swear'st grace o'erboard, not an oath on shore?
Hast thou no mouth by land? What is the news?   220

Boatswain The best news is that we have safely
    found
Our king and company; the next, our ship,
Which, but three glasses since, we gave out split,
Is tight and yare and bravely rigged as when
We first put out to sea.   225

Ariel   [*Aside to* PROSPERO] Sir, all this service
Have I done since I went.

Prospero   [*Aside to* ARIEL] My tricksy spirit!

Alonso These are not natural events; they
    strengthen
From strange to stranger. Say, how came you hither?

Boatswain If I did think, sir, I were well awake,
I'd strive to tell you. We are dead of sleep   230
And (how we know not) all clapped under hatches;
Where, but even now, with strange and several
    noises
Of roaring, shrieking, howling, jingling chains,
And moe diversity of sounds, all horrible,
We were awaked; straightway at liberty;   235
Where we, in all her trim, freshly beheld
Our royal, good, and gallant ship, our master

---

213.   *his own:* i.e., in control of himself and his destiny.

214.   *still:* forever.

217.   *prophesied:* predicted (in Act I, Scene 1).

218.   *blasphemy:* i.e., you blasphemous man.

219.   *swear'st . . . o'erboard:* drives God's grace overboard by swearing.

223.   *glasses:* hour-glasses.

224.   *yare:* shipshape.

226.   *tricksy:* tricky, clever.

227.   *strengthen:* grow.

234.   *moe:* more.

235.   *straightway at liberty:* immediately set free.

236.   *trim:* sail.

Cap'ring to eye her. On a trice, so please you.
Even in a dream, were we divided from them
And were brought moping hither.

Ariel   [*Aside to* PROSPERO] Was't well done? 240

Prospero [*Aside to* ARIEL] Bravely, my diligence.
     Thou shalt be free.

Alonso This is as strange a maze as e'er men trod,
     And there is in this business more than nature
     Was ever conduct of. Some oracle
     Must rectify our knowledge.   245

Prospero   Sir, my liege,
     Do not infest your mind with beating on
     The strangeness of this business: at picked leisure,
     Which shall be shortly, single I'll resolve you
     (Which to you shall seem probable) of every
     These happened accidents; till when, be cheerful   250
     And think of each thing well. [*Aside to* ARIEL] Come
     hither, spirit.
     Set Caliban and his companions free.
     Untie the spell. [*Exit* ARIEL.] How fares my gracious
         sir.
     There are yet missing of your company
     Some few odd lads that you remember not.   255

Enter ARIEL, *driving in* CALIBAN, STEPHANO, *and*
     TRINCULO *in their stolen apparel.*

Stephano Every man shift for all the rest, and let
     no man take care of himself; for all is but fortune.
     Coragio bully-monster, coragio!

Trinculo If these be true spies which I wear in my
     head, here's a goodly sight.   260

Caliban O Setebos, these be brave spirits indeed!
     How fine my master is! I am afraid
     He will chastise me.

Sebastian   Ha, ha!
     What things are these, my Lord Antonio?
     Will money buy 'em?   265

Antonio   Very like. One of them
     Is a plain fish and no doubt marketable.

---

238.   *Cap'ring:* dancing for joy.

        on a trice: in an instant.

240.   *moping:* in a trance or daze.

244.   *conduct of:* the conductor of.

245.   *liege:* lord.

246.   *infest:* trouble.

247.   *at picked leisure:* when convenient.

248.   *single:* both by myself and in one telling.

        resolve: explain.

256.   *Every man . . . himself:* Stephano's drunk inversion
        of "All for one and one for all."

258.   *Coragio:* courage (Italian).

262.   *fine:* i.e., finely dressed in his costume as Duke of
        Milan.

Prospero Mark but the badges of these men, my
    lords,
Then say if they be true. This misshapen knave,
His mother was a witch, and one so strong
That could control the moon, make flows and ebbs,   270
And deal in her command without her power.
These three have robbed me, and this demi-devil
(For he's a bastard one) had plotted with them
To take my life. Two of these fellows you
Must know and own; this thing of darkness I   275
Acknowledge mine.

Caliban   I shall be pinched to death.

Alonso Is not this Stephano, my drunken butler?

Sebastian He is drunk now: where had he wine?

Alonso And Trinculo is reeling ripe: where should they
Find this grand liquor that hath gilded 'em?   280
How cam'st thou in this pickle?

Trinculo I have been in such a pickle, since I saw
you last, that I fear me will never out of my bones. I
shall not fear fly-blowing.

Sebastian Why, how now, Stephano?   285

Stephano O, touch me not! I am not Stephano, but
a cramp.

Prospero You'ld be king o' the isle, sirrah?

Stephano I should have been a sore one then.

Alonso This is a strange thing as e'er I looked on.   290

Prospero He is as disproportioned in his manners
As in his shape. Go, sirrah, to my cell;
Take with you your companions. As you look
To have my pardon, trim it handsomely.

Caliban Ay, that I will; and I'll be wise hereafter,   295
And seek for grace. What a thrice-double ass
Was I to take this drunkard for a god
And worship this dull fool!

Prospero   Go to! Away!

---

267. *badges:* signs worn by servants, indicating whom they served.

268. *true:* honest.

270. *flows and ebbs:* i.e., of the tides.

271. *her . . . her:* Sycorax could dabble in the moon's power but to fully command the moon was beyond Sycorax's power.

279. *reeling ripe:* staggering and smelling from drink.

280. *gilded:* flushed, made brighter in color than usual.

282. *pickle:* in the senses of (1) mess, predicament, (2) preservative (either the liquor he has drunk, or the horsepond).

284. *fly-blowing:* i.e., since he is pickled, he will not decay as other meat does.

288. *sirrah:* little sir; a term of disrespect.

289. *sore:* bad, inadequate.

294. *trim it:* clean and decorate the cell.

296. *grace:* pardon, favor.

Alonso Hence, and bestow your luggage where
    you found it.

Sebastian Or stole it rather.   300

[*Exeunt* CALIBAN, STEPHANO, *and* TRINCULO.]

Prospero Sir, I invite your Highness and your train
    To my poor cell, where you shall take your rest
    For this one night; which, part of it, I'll waste
    With such discourse as, I not doubt, shall make it
    Go quickly away — the story of my life,   305
    And the particular accidents gone by
    Since I came to this isle; and in the morn
    I'll bring you to your ship, and so to Naples,
    Where I have hope to see the nuptial
    Of these our dear-beloved solemnized;   310
    And thence retire me to my Milan, where
    Every third thought shall be my grave.

Alonso   I long
    To hear the story of your life, which must
    Take the ear strangely.

Prospero   I'll deliver all;
    And promise you calm seas, auspicious gales,   315
    And sail so expeditious that shall catch
    Your royal fleet far off. — My Ariel, chick,
    That is thy charge. Then to the elements
    Be free, and fare thou well! — Please you draw
      near. *Exeunt omnes.*

EPILOGUE

(Spoken by Prospero)
    Now my charms are all o'verthrown,
    And what strength I have's mine own,
    Which is most faint. Now 'tis true
    I must be here confined by you
    Or sent to Naples. Let me not,   5
    Since I have my dukedom got
    And pardoned the deceiver, dwell
    In this bare island by your spell;
    But release me from my bands
    With the help of your good hands.   10
    Gentle breath of yours my sails,

---

299. *luggage:* the stolen garments (from Act IV, Scene 1).

303. *waste:* occupy, fill up.

306. *accidents:* events.

312. *Every third . . . grave:* perhaps the other two thoughts will be for Miranda and Milan; or perhaps the meaning is simply that Prospero will give much thought to death.

314. *deliver:* recount, relate.

315. *auspicious gales:* fortunate winds.

316. *sail:* sailing.

    expeditious: swift.

    catch: catch up with.

4. *confined by you:* Prospero hands his magical authority over to the audience.

8. *your spell:* i.e., your silence, lack of applause.

9. *bands:* bonds; Prospero means that he cannot leave the stage until they have applauded him with their "good hands."

11. *gentle breath:* both cheers and favorable comments to others about the play

Must fill, or else my project fails,
Which was to please. Now I want
Spirits to enforce, art to enchant;
And my ending is despair   15
Unless I be relieved by prayer,
Which pierces so that it assaults
Mercy itself and frees all faults.
As you from crimes would pardoned be,
Let your indulgence set me free. *Exit.*   20

13. *want:* lack.

16. *prayer:* hands folded together as in prayer, only repeatedly, to produce applause.

20. *indulgence:* leniency, forgiveness.

COMMENTARY

It is not generally considered good stagecraft for characters to exit and reenter without any other action taking place. That Prospero and Ariel do so here is often taken as a signal that when Shakespeare's company, the King's Men, performed the play, a break was observed between the fourth and fifth acts, possibly to trim the candles or replace the torches that provided lighting indoors.

Prospero is shortly to gather all his enemies together and confront them. In his dialogue with Ariel stands the edge on which the driving question of this play's formulaic type truly balances: Is this a revenge tragedy or a romantic comedy?

Ariel describes the "distracted" magical trance, in which we shortly see the court party as they enter. Ariel is particularly passionate in describing the "Good old Lord Gonzalo, "who has been so moved by the punishments Prospero has already enforced on Alonso that "tears run down his beard like winter's drops / From eaves of reeds" (lines 16–17). Ariel's assertion that, were he human, he would pity and forgive the three men of sin is the deciding factor in Prospero's decision to do the same.

As Prospero then goes on to explain his decision, Shakespeare draws once again on Montaigne for words and ideas. Montaigne writes in his essay "Of Cruelty":

He that through a natural facility and genuine mildness should neglect or contemn injuries received should no doubt perform a rare action, and worthy commendation. But he who, being touched and stung to the quick, should arm himself with reason against this furiously-blind desire of revenge, and in the end, after a great conflict, yield himself master over it, should doubtless do much more. (*The Complete Essays of Montaigne*, trans. David M. Frame. Stanford, 1957)

Shakespeare collapses and condenses these thoughts into Prospero's self-realization that his reason and his potential to exercise mercy and forgiveness is far more noble than his desires for retribution. Prospero resolves to forgive all, to give up magic, and to set Ariel free.

As Ariel exits to usher in the court party, Prospero begins the process of forsaking the magic arts, calling on the spirits of Nature one last time and recounting his previous accomplishments in magic. His account is also a reminder that Prospero is a practitioner of so-called "white magic," which deals with the manipulation of Nature and natural elements as opposed to necromancy or "black magic," which deals with devils, demons, and the Supernatural.

Shakespeare draws on a speech from the Roman poet Ovid here. The speech was well known to Shakespeare and his audience in Arthur Golding's 1567 translation of the Latin original. As with his treatment of Montaigne earlier in the scene, Shakespeare proves a master of condensing and reworking the words and ideas of his source materials to heighten their dramatic and thematic power. A direct comparison of Golding's translation with Shakespeare's adaptation demonstrates this power:

> . . . ye elves of hills, of brooks, of woods alone
> Of standing lakes, and of the night, approach ye every one,
> Through help of whom (the crooked banks much wondering at the thing)
> I have compelled streams to run clean backward to their spring.
> By charms I make the calm seas round and make the rough seas plain,
> And cover all the sky with clouds, and chase them thence again.
> By charms I raise and lay the winds, and burst the viper's jaw,
> And from the bowels of the earth both stones and trees do draw.
> Whole woods and forests I remove; I make the mountains shake,
> And even the earth itself to groan and fearfully to quake.
> I call up dead men from their graves and thee,
> O lightsome moon, I darken oft, thought beaten brass abate thy peril soon;
> Our sorcery dims the morning fair and darks the sun at noon.

(from Ovid's *Metamorphoses* Book Vii, lines 197–209. *The XV Books of P. Ovidius Naso, entytuled Metamorphoses*, trans. Arthur Golding. London, 1567)

Of immediate improvement is Shakespeare's abandonment of Golding's meter. Golding's translation is written in *Alexendrines* or *fourteeners*, lines of poetry with fourteen syllables or seven metric feet. Shakespeare adapts this to his traditional meter, iambic pentameter, a line of five metric feet or ten syllables. In addition to removing the clumsiness of the verse, Shakespeare also removes much of the clumsiness of the imagery.

Although Ovid's lines already have a highly visual quality to them, Shakespeare, in adapting them, improves on both the visual and aural aspects of the language. The harnessed power of Nature as a potentially violent and destructive force is given compact description by Shakespeare as the "roaring war . . . twixt the green sea and azured vault" — between sea and sky.

Many commentators read these lines, with the promise that, at the end of the magical work, Prospero will break his staff and drown his book, as Shakespeare's farewell to the theatrical arts. Although this is an attractive idea, there is little support for it. In all likelihood, this was the last play authored by Shakespeare on his own, but not his last play. Two later plays, *Henry VIII* and *The Two Noble Kinsmen*, are generally believed to have been co-authored by Shakespeare and John Fletcher, the playwright who would replace Shakespeare as the

"*Here Prospero discovers Ferdinand and Miranda, playing at chess*" (V.1 Stage Direction). When Prospero reveals to Alonso that Alonso's son, Ferdinand, is miraculously alive in the play's final scene, he reveals the Prince to be playing chess with Miranda. The game was undoubtedly chosen by Shakespeare specifically for its connections to ideas of strategy, political maneuvering, and dynasty.

principal playwright for the King's Men.

A perhaps more practical understanding of Shakespeare's intentions is to understand Prospero as a figure who in part represents King James I. King James, like Prospero, was a father, a temporal lord or governor, and a scholar. Importantly, James wrote a book on *Daemonologie* that was published in 1597. In it, he warns against the power of belief in devils, witchcraft, and sorcery. Prospero is, like James, a scholarly magician and not a practitioner of the sort of necromancy or black magic that James specifically wrote against in his book.

James was not ashamed to think of himself as a scholar and a source of wisdom for his people. Prospero, clearly, is the same way. Recall that in Act I, Scene 2, he informs his daughter that he was "so reputed / In dignity, and for the liberal Arts / Without a parallel" (I.2.72–74). Although Shakespeare is almost certainly flattering King James with his presentation of Prospero, he is perhaps also sending a mild warning that effective governors, while they are learned, should not become so wrapped up in their own studies and their own affairs that they cease to care for and actually govern their subjects.

Ariel ushers in the court party, still wrapped in a magical trance. Prospero addresses each of them individually, beginning with Gonzalo. Gonzalo, who is and always has been noble, merits Prospero's sympathies. It was never Prospero's intention to punish Gonzalo. Although Alonso has earlier expressed a sense of repentance (in believing he heard Prospero's name pronounced by the thunder following the banquet), Antonio and Sebastian show no remorse.

After the spell is lifted and the court party is again able to see, speak, and interact with Prospero (now dressed in garments appropriate to his position as Duke of Milan and not in his magical robes), they are amazed.

"This is a strange a thing as e'er I looked on" (V.1.289). The strangeness and wonder of the play is carried through to the play's final scene as discovery upon discovery is unfolded, culminating in the entry of the drunken comic trio of Caliban (shown here), Stephano, and Trinculo.

Sebastian, as a sign of his lack of repentance, believes the vision of Prospero to be a devil, a product of black magic. Antonio says nothing, leaving an awkward tension in the scene, because one of the preconditions of forgiveness is, of course, repentance.

The only figure who is genuinely repentant is Alonso. (Gonzalo, after all, has nothing for which he needs to repent.) Prospero plays on Alonso's sorrow by suggesting that the storm has likewise robbed him of a child. Doing so increases the dramatic value (for Alonso, at least) of the discovery of Miranda and Ferdinand playing chess.

There is deliberate significance to the game of chess: it is one of strategy and dynasty and frequently called upon as a metaphor for the political struggles of Kings and countries. There is also significance in the way they play it: Miranda accuses Ferdinand of cheating (like father like son?) but allows him to get away with it. In this loving banter, Shakespeare reveals the hopeful direction of the future and the fact that Miranda, armed with the lessons of her father, will indeed bring about a regeneration and a redemption of the older generation in marrying Ferdinand.

Miranda's optimism explodes in her proclamation, "O brave new world / That has such people in't!" (lines 183–184). Although Prospero sarcastically qualifies this, the hopeful promise and sense of wonder that Miranda represents is undiminished.

This sense of wonderment and hope is echoed in Gonzalo's lyrical reflection that in essence summarizes the overarching redemptive theme of regeneration and discovery at the heart of the play. Through tests, trials, tempests, and wanderings, a questioning of self emerges, and with that questioning a sense that no man was his own; but this period of trial is temporary and now the rightful Milan is replaced and a fruitful dynastic marriage secured, to carry forth stability and happiness to future generations.

The play comes full circle with the reappearance of the Boatswain. Gonzalo's observation that this man would die on dry land has, at least temporarily, proven correct. In the return of these characters, the tightness of the play's structure and its strict adherence to the unity of time and place is underscored.

The only remaining characters not yet brought to the reunion (and to forgiveness) are Caliban and his coconspirators. Although still drunk, they are indeed repentant. Stephano swears off drink; Trinculo already knows he will feel the effects of this drunken spree for some time to come. Caliban is genuinely repentant and introspective; he admits his foolishness. He is forgiven, and at long last recognized by Prospero: "This thing of darkness I / Acknowledge mine" (lines 275–276).

Prospero promises to tell the full story of his life on the island and to attend the court party in a return journey to Milan. All that remains is to set Ariel free, which Prospero promises to do. Ariel's only remaining task is to provide fair weather for the return journey to Italy.

Epilogue

Although Prospero's final lines at the end of Act V, "Pray you, draw near," is clearly an invitation to the actors onstage to withdraw into his "full poor cell," it is also an invitation to the audience as a lead-in to the Epilogue.

John Cassevetes, Gena Rowlands, and Molly Ringwald in the 1982 film, The Tempest, *loosely based on Shakespeare's play.*
Everett Collection

The form of the Epilogue follows an established tradition (look for an example in the Epilogue delivered by Puck in *A Midsummer Night's Dream*) in which the actor delivering it both apologizes for the limitations of the play just performed and asks the audience for applause. Prospero's Epilogue also addresses thematic importance as well. He focuses on forgiveness, turning over his power of magic and containment to the audience and pleading with them to set him free. Eager readers might well also read into Prospero's use of the terms "pardon" and "indulgence," references to Roman Catholicism. Ultimately, such a reading stands on a flimsy foundation, however, as the better understanding of Prospero is as representation of the Protestant King James and, thus, through his actions of control, instruction, and forgiveness, presents a model for kingship that James would no doubt have seen as a compliment.

Notes

The Tempest

CLIFFSCOMPLETE REVIEW

Use this CliffsComplete Review to gauge what you've learned and to build confidence in your understanding of the original text. After you work through the review questions, the problem-solving exercises, and the suggested activities, you're well on your way to understanding and appreciating the works of William Shakespeare.

IDENTIFY THE QUOTATION

Identify the following quotations by answering these questions:

* Who is the speaker of the quote?
* What does it reveal about the speaker's character?
* What does it tell us about other characters within the play?
* Where does it occur within the play?
* What does it show us about the themes of the play?
* What significant imagery do you see in the quote, and how do these images relate to the overall imagery of the play?

1. His tears run down his beard like winter's drops
   From eaves of reeds. Your charm so strongly
         works 'em
   That if you now beheld them, your affections
   Would become tender.

2. You were kneeled to and importuned otherwise
   By all of us; and the fair soul herself
   Weighed between loathness and obedience, at
   Which end o' th' beam should bow. We have
         lost your son,
   I fear forever. Milan and Naples have
   More widows in them of this business' making
   Than we bring men to comfort them. The
         fault's your own.

3. They are both in either's powers; but this swift
         business
   I must uneasy make, lest too light winning
   Make the prize light.

4. Full fathom five thy father lies,
   Of his bones are coral made;
   Those are pearls that were his eyes;
   Nothing of him that doth fade,
   But doth suffer a sea-change
   Into something rich and strange.

5. As wicked dew as e'er my mother brushed
   With raven's feather from unwholsome fen
   Drop on you both! A south-west blow on ye
   And blister you all over!

6. If he were that which now he's like — that's
         dead —
   Whom I with this obedient steel, three inches
         of it,
   Can lay to bed for ever; whiles you, doing thus,
   To the perpetual wink for aye might put
   This ancient morsel, this Sir Prudence.

7. A devil, a born devil on whose nature
Nurture can never stick; on whom my pains,
Humanely taken, all, all lost, quite lost;
And as with age his body uglier grows,
So his mind cankers. I will plague them all,
Even unto roaring.

8. Be not afeard, this isle is full of noises,
Sounds and sweet airs, that give delight and
hurt not.
Sometimes a thousand twangling instruments
Will hum about mine ears; and sometime
voices,
That if I then had waked after long sleep,
Will make me sleep again; and then in
dreaming,
The clouds me thought would open, and show
riches
Ready to drop upon me, that when I waked
I cried to dream again.

9. This was well done, my bird!
Thy shape invisible retain thou still.
The trumpery in my house, go bring it hither
For stale to catch these thieves.

10. My spirits, as in a dream, are all bound up.
My father's loss, the weakness which I feel,
the wrack of all my friends, or this man's
threats,
To whom I am subdued, are but light to me,
Might I but through my prison once a day
Behold this maid.

TRUE/FALSE

1. T F Stephano, Trinculo, and Caliban are drunk on beer.

2. T F Miranda was approximately three years old when she and Prospero first arrived on the island.

3. T F When Prospero and Miranda arrive on the island, Caliban is its only inhabitant.

4. T F Prospero is a practioner of black magic.

5. T F Sebastian rejects Antonio's suggestion that they plot to kill Alonso, Sebastian's brother.

6. T F Caliban once attempted to rape Miranda.

7. T F Gonzalo is the wronged Duke of Milan.

8. T F Trinculo is a brave knight who serves Prospero.

9. T F Prospero is pleased that Ferdinand and Miranda fall in love at first sight.

10. T F A magical banquet distracts Stephano and Trinculo from their plot to murder Prospero.

11. T F The Boatswain and Master both drown in the shipwreck that begins the play.

12. T F The Masque in Act IV represents Winter or Death.

13. T F Ariel was once a prisoner in a pine tree for twelve years.

14. T F Prospero and Miranda have lived on the island for twelve years.

15. T F Antonio begs Prospero for forgiveness in the play's final scene.

MULTIPLE CHOICE

1. Ferdinand is the son of:

   a. Prospero

   b. Antonio

   c. Sebastian

   d. Alonso

2. Miranda is the daughter of:

   a. Prospero

   b. Antonio

   c. Sebastian

   d. Alonso

3. The play takes place

   a. in Milan

   b. in Naples

   c. on an island

   d. in London

4. Ferdinand describes hauling fireword as

   a. painful pleasure

   b. easy work

   c. torture

   d. shame

5. Alonso is in a foul mood in Act II, Scene 1, because

   a. Antonio has insulted him

   b. Sebastian has struck him

   c. he believes his son is drowned

   d. Gonzalo stepped on his toe

6. What is the "Some vanity of mine art" Prospero commands Ariel to provide for Ferdinand and Miranda?

   a. a thunderstorm

   b. a masque

   c. a banquet

   d. a puppet show

7. What distracts Stephano and Trinculo from their plot to murder Prospero?

   a. a thunderstorm

   b. a masque

   c. a banquet

   d. glittering costumes

8. Who proclaims "O brave new world / That has such people in't"?

   a. Miranda

   b. Ferdinand

   c. Caliban

   d. Gonzalo

9. What does Prospero ask for from the audience in the Epilogue?

   a. forgiveness

   b. money

   c. applause

   d. a and c

10. Who does Caliban claim is the rightful master of the island?

   a. Prospero

   b. Ariel

   c. Stephano

   d. Caliban

11. Who aided Prospero and Miranda by supplying them with food and other necessities when they were put to sea?

   a. Adrian

   b. Gonzalo

   c. Alonso

   d. Sebastian

12. Who believes the air on the island "breathes upon us here most sweetly"?

   a. Adrian

   b. Ferdinand

   c. Francisco

   d. Gonazalo

13. Who argues that Ferdinand "beat the surges under him" and "came alive to land"?

   a. Adrian

   b. Sebastian

   c. Francisco

   d. Gonazalo

14. Who aided Antonio in his ousting of Prospero?

   a. Adrian

   b. Sebastian

   c. Alonso

   d. Gonzalo

15. To whom does Prospero give the command, "then to the elements / Be free and fare thou well"?

   a. Caliban

   b. Ariel

   c. Miranda

   d. Gonzalo

FILL IN THE BLANK

1. Prospero is the Duke of _____ and Alonso is the King of _____, two city-states in the country of _____.

2. _____ is Prospero's spirit-like helper and _____ is his earthy slave.

3. Sycorax, Caliban's mother, is said to be a _____.

4. When Prospero first arrives on the island, he sets Ariel free from a _____.

5. When Ariel misbehaves, Prospero threatens to imprison Ariel in a _____.

6. Caliban warns Stephano that before killing Prospero, Stephano must possess Prospero's _____.

7. Caliban describes _____ as a - nonpareil.

8. Ariel, as a Harpy, presents a _____ in Act III, Scene 3.

9. Ariel accuses _____, _____, and _____ of being "three men of sin" in Act III, Scene 3.

10. Near the end of the play, Prospero promises to break _____ and drown _____.

DISCUSSION

Use the following questions to generate discussion:

1. "By Providence Divine": To what extent is Providence (Fate, Fortune, Destiny) the controlling force of this play? To what extent is human action or agency in control?

2. "This island's mine": Who, in your view, is the rightful ruler of the island? What does Shakespeare seem to be saying about monarchy (kingship) and government in this play?

3. "If a virgin, / And your affections not gone forth, I'll make you / The Queen of Naples": Prospero seems obsessed with protecting Miranda's virginity. Is he? If so, how or why is his concern warranted?

4. "on whose nature / Nurture can never stick": What is the relationship between Art and Nature in the play?

5. What comment on colonialism does Shakespeare appear to be making in this play? Does he justify it or attack it?

6. "O you wonder": Discuss the importance of magic and the power of wonder in this play.

7. "The government I cast upon my brother": Is Prospero guilty of being criminally irresponsible or negligent as the governor of Milan? Is Antonio justified in removing him from office?

8. "Had I plantation of this isle": What do you make of Gonzalo's proposal for an ideal commonwealth or utopia in Act II, Scene 1, lines 139–164? Do you agree or disagree with his vision of a perfect society? Is it practical?

9. "The isle is full of noises, / Sounds and sweet airs that give delight and hurt not": Discuss the importance of music and song in the play.

10. "O Brave New World": What is the importance of setting to your understanding of the play? Does Prospero's island represent America? Does a precise location for the island need to be known in order to fully understand the play?

IDENTIFYING PLAY ELEMENTS

Find examples of the following elements in the text of *The Tempest*:

* Alliteration (repetition of speech sounds in a sequence of nearby words)
* Metonymy (the literal term for one thing is used as a symbol for something with which it is closely associated)
* Rhetorical questions (question asked not for an actual reply but to create a stronger emphasis than a direct statement)
* Personification (a non-human object is described with the characteristics of a person)
* Sarcasm (apparent praise used as a form of insult)
* Allusion (reference to other literature)
* Dirge (short, informal expression of grief on the occasion of someone's death)
* Monologue (a speech delivered by one person)
* Stock character (character types that conform, at least in part, to a pattern from earlier works)
* Slapstick or physical humor

ACTIVITIES

The following activities can springboard you into further discussions and projects:

1. With a partner, improvise a scene in which one person attempts to talk the other into doing something both of you know is wrong. Switch roles and improvise a new situation.

2. Imagine you have gone on a camping trip and fallen asleep in the woods. When you awake, the forest has been magically transformed into a psychedelic array of colors, and with everything either enlarged or otherwise looking strange and transformed. React, without words and without physical reaction to other people, to your new environment.

3. Draw a line on a piece of paper and label one end "most loved by Prospero" and the other "most hated by Prospero." Place each of the characters in their appropriate place on the continuum. Try the same activity with different labels for each end of the line, such as:

* youngest to oldest

* most evil to most moral

* character I like the most to character I dislike the most

* part I'd most like to play to part I'd least like to play

(Adapted from Rex Gibson, Cambridge School Shakespeare edition of *The Tempest*)

4. In pairs, take the parts of Prospero and Ariel and read through the lines assigned to each character for Act I, Scene 2, lines 242–350. How does Ariel present his/her case for freedom? How does Prospero respond? Does either character change (grow more angry or back down) as the exchange progresses?

5. In groups of three, stage the scene from Act II, Scene 2, in which Caliban, Trinculo, and Stephano first meet. What do you do to distinguish the way each of these characters speaks? How do the lines need to be delivered and what physical action must take place according to the details in the text and in order to make the audience laugh?

6. Create an imaginative, newspaper-style report on the ouster of Prospero. The play only presents his version of the story; as an investigative reporter, reconstruct the views of Antonio, Alonso, and Gonzalo concerning the events Prospero describes in Act I, Scene 2.

7. Choose a short scene — or a section of a larger scene — of approximately 100 lines. Provide detailed directions for actors, designers, and theatre technicians on how you would stage the scene. You may wish to include diagrams showing your design for the stage set, costumes, and special effects.

8. A *Utopia* is an ideal society; Gonzalo describes his in Act II, Scene 1. Describe your own ideal society. How is it governed? What is valued or important? What is not allowed? Be as descriptive as possible. When you have finished, look up the word *Utopia* in a dictionary. Does its meaning — especially its original Latin meaning — leave you feeling disappointed or encouraged?

9. Read again through the wedding masque in Act IV, Scene 1. Draw illustrations of Iris, Ceres, Juno, and the nymphs and reapers, based on the descriptions of them in the text.

10. In England, a weekly radio program called *Desert Island Discs* asks famous people what eight pieces of music they would want with them if shipwrecked on a desert island. They are also allowed to imagine that they may bring one book and one luxury item with them (the Bible and the complete works of Shakespeare are already on the island). Choose one or more of the characters from the play and write, as a script, the contents of an interview with them in which they reveal their musical, literary, and luxury choices.

ANSWERS

Identify the Quotation

1. Speaker: Ariel; Person spoken to: Prospero; Location: Act V, Scene 1

2. Speaker: Sebastian; Person spoken to: Alonso; Location: Act II, Scene 1

3. Speaker: Prospero; Person spoken to: Audience; Location: Act I, Scene 2

4. Speaker: Ariel; Person spoken to: Ferdinand; Location: Act I, Scene 2

5. Speaker: Caliban; Persons spoken to: Prospero and Miranda; Location: Act I, Scene 2

6. Speaker: Antonio; Person spoken to: Sebastian; Location: Act II, Scene 1

7. Speaker: Prospero (describing Caliban); Person spoken to: Audience; Location: Act IV, Scene 1

8. Speaker: Caliban; Persons spoken to: Stephano and Trinculo; Location: Act III, Scene 2

9. Speaker: Prospero; Person spoken to: Ariel; Location: Act IV, Scene 1

10. Speaker: Ferdinand; Person spoken to: Audience/Self; Location: Act I, Scene 2

True/False

1. False 2. True 3. False 4. False 5. False 6. True
7. False 8. False 9. True 10. False 11. False
12. False 13. True 14. True 15. False

Multiple Choice

1. d. 2. a. 3. c. 4. a. 5. c. 6. b. 7. d. 8. a. 9. a.
10. a. 11. b. 12. a. 13. c. 14. c. 15. b.

Fill in the Blank

1. Milan; Naples; Italy 2. Ariel; Caliban
3. witch 4. pine tree 5. oak tree 6. books
7. Miranda 8. banquet 9. Antonio; Sebastian;
Alonso 10. his staff; his book

CLIFFSCOMPLETE RESOURCE CENTER

The learning doesn't need to stop here. CliffsComplete Resource Center shows you the best of the best: great links to information in print, on film, and online. And the following aren't all the great resources available to you; visit **www.cliffsnotes.com** for tips on reading literature, writing papers, giving presentations, locating other resources, and testing your knowledge.

BOOKS

Bate, Jonathan. *The Genius of Shakespeare*. New York: Oxford University Press, 1998.

A thorough survey of many of the myths, anecdotes, and mystery surrounding Shakespeare and his career.

Bentley, Gerald Eades. *The Profession of Dramatist in Shakespeare's Time, 1590–1642*. Princeton: Princeton University Press, 1971.

A thorough and detailed analysis of the economic and social conditions of sixteenth- and seventeenth-century playwrights.

————. *The Profession of Player in Shakespeare's Time, 1590–1642*. Princeton, Princeton University Press, 1984.

A thorough and detailed analysis of the economic and social conditions of sixteenth- and seventeenth-century actors.

Blake, Norman F. *Shakespeare's Language: An Introduction*. New York: St. Martin's, 1983.

A useful introduction into some of the complexities of Early Modern English.

Bullough, Geoffrey, ed. *Narrative and Dramatic Sources of Shakespeare*. 8 vols. London: Routledge & Kegan Paul, 1957–1975.

Bullough's monumental piece of scholarship gathers together sources and analogues for all of Shakespeare's plays. *The Tempest* materials are presented in the eighth and final volume.

Chute, Marchette. *Shakespeare of London*. London: Martin Secker and Warburg, 1951.

A highly readable biography of Shakespeare. Recently reprinted by Barnes and Noble Books.

Clark, Sandra. *The Tempest* [Penguin Critical Studies Series]. New York: Penguin, 1986.

An overview of critical interpretations of themes and issues in the play. This volume is part of the highly readable Penguin Critical Studies Series on individual Shakespearean plays.

Dollimore, Jonathan and Alan Sinfeld, eds. *Political Shakespeare: New Essays in Cultural Materialism*. Ithaca: Cornell University Press, 1985.

A study of Shakespeare's plays as statements on sixteenth- and seventeenth-century politics. Explores political power as it attempts to control, consolidate, and subvert power from other sources.

Frye, Northrop. *A Natural Perspective: The Development of Shakespearean Comedy and Romance.* New York: Columbia University Press, 1965.

This study explores the way in which the structures of Shakespeare's plays provide insight into their moral content.

_____. *Anatomy of Criticism.* New York, Athenaeum, 1968.

A theoretical essay on the nature of comedy as it relates to core myths or timeless stories.

Greenblatt, Stephen. *Shakespearean Negotiations: The Circulation of Social Energy in Renaissance England.* Berkeley: Univeristy of Californa Press, 1988.

This highly influential book provides a "New Historicist" approach to Shakespeare and his use of sources including, but not limited to, printed texts and other forms of communications. The core theories are similar to those explored in Dollimore and Sinfeld's *Political Shakespeare.*

Kay, Carol M. and Henry E. Jacobs, eds. *Shakespeare's Romances Reconsidered.* Lincoln: University of Nebraska Press, 1978.

A collection of 11 essays including a survey of critical approaches and a bibliography of more than 600 items.

Kermode, Frank, ed. *The Tempest* [The Arden Shakespeare, Second Series]. 1954. London: Routledge, 1987.

Kermode's introduction remains one of the most thorough and detailed explorations of the sources, textual authority, and major themes of *The Tempest* available.

Knight, G. Wilson. *The Crown of Life: Essays in the Interpreatiton of Shakespeare's Final Plays.* London: Oxford University Press, 1930.

Wilson Knight's study is a classic, stressing the power of intuition and imagination in understanding the total poetic experience of Shakespeare's late plays.

Langbaum, Robert, ed. *The Tempest* [The Signet Classic Shakespeare]. 1964. New York: Penguin, 1998.

Includes a superb selection of critical essays and detailed recommendations of further reading.

Muir, Kenneth. *Shakespeare's Sources: Comedies and Tragedies.* London: Methuen, 1957.

Muir provides some commentary on Shakespeare's use and manipulation of his sources in twenty plays. A thorough and clear but now somewhat dated analysis.

Palmer, D.J., ed. *Shakespeare:* The Tempest *A Casebook.* London: Macmillan, 1968.

A collection of essays from the seventeenth century to the present.

Schoenbaum, Sam. *William Shakespeare: A Documentary Life.* Oxford: Oxford University Press, 1975.

A detailed analysis of the existing documents from Shakespeare's lifetime providing information about him. Contains reproductions of original documents.

Thomson, Peter. *Shakespeare's Professional Career.* Cambridge: Cambridge University Press, 1992.

Similar to Bentley's book on the profession of dramatist, but with specific focus and interpretation of Shakespeare's experience as a professional playwright.

_____. *Shakespeare's Theatre.* New York: Routledge, second ed. 1992.

A very readable and useful introduction to the operations of theatres during Shakespeare's day.

Tillyard, E.M.W. *Shakespeare: The Last Plays*. London: Chatto & Windus, 1938.

Tillyard explores in detail the complicated relationship of the late plays to tragedy and tragic patterns.

Traversi, Derek. *Shakespeare: The Last Phase*. Stanford: Stanford University Press, 1955.

Detailed analysis of all of the late plays or romances with a particular concentration on their shared use of breakdown and reconciliation as the core of their structure and thematic importance.

Vaughan, Virginia Mason, and Alden T. Vaughan, eds. *The Tempest* [Arden Shakespeare, Third Series]. Walton-on-Thames: Thompson, 1999.

This superb new edition is, and will remain for some time, the scholarly standard. The introduction provides far more detailed discussion of sources, critical commentary, and onstage presentation of the play than space allows in this CliffsComplete. Lengthy excerpts from the sources are printed as appendices.

_____. *Critical Essays on Shakespeare's* The Tempest. New York: G.K. Hall & Co., 1998.

An outstanding collection of essays interpreting the sources, performances, and criticism of *The Tempest*.

Wells, Stanley, ed. *The Cambridge Companion to Shakespeare Studies*. Cambridge, Cambridge University Press, 1986.

A helpful introduction to various aspects of Shakespeare studies and collection of recommendations for further reading.

_____. *Shakespeare: An Illustrated Dictionary*. Oxford: Oxford University Press, 1985.

A condensed and helpful guide to a variety of topics and terms, with illustrations.

INTERNET

Mr. William Shakespeare and the Internet

daphne.palomar.edu/shakespeare/

The place to start on the Internet for information on Shakespeare. "Mr. William Shakespeare and the Internet" has a wealth of scholarly and general interest resources and numerous links to both online texts, background information, and other sites concerned with Shakespeare.

Shakespeare Illustrated

www.cc.emory.edu/english/classes/shakespeare_
illustrated/shakespeare.html

Explore this site for visuals either of Shakespeare or his plays.

Shakespeare's Plays: Lesson Plans and Resources

miningco.com/education/7-12educators/msub109drama.htm

Teachers, in particular, can find helpful resources at this Web site. The site provides links to a variety of sites concerned with teaching materials for several of Shakespeare's plays, including a highly useful teaching guide published by Penguin Books.

Shakespeare Trivia Game

rocketdownload.com/details/stra/shak.htm

A Shakespeare trivia game (not specific to *The Tempest*) can be downloaded for a free thirty-day trial from this Web site.

FILMS

Forbidden Planet (1956). Dir. Fred McLeod Wilcox.

A science-fiction adaptation of basic elements of *The Tempest* story include a Prospero-like figure named Dr. Morbeus and his Miranda-like daughter Altera. With the assistance of Robby the Robot, Morbeus' creation, the Morbeus has established his own empire with himself as its ruler on this otherwise more-or-less uninhabited planet.

The Tempest (1979). Dir. Derek Jarman.

A visually lush and artistic filming of the play. Difficult to find in video stores, however.

The Tempest (1980). Dir. John Gorrie.

This is the BBC version of the play, in period costume. An accurate representation but also less inventive than Jarman's presentation.

Tempest (1982*)*. Dir. Paul Mazursky.

A dark comedy loosely based on Shakespeare's play with a Prospero-like character named Philip Demetrius. Philip undergoes a midlife crisis and leaves New York City for a Mediterranean island paradise with his daughter, Miranda, after his wife, Antonia, begins an affair with his boss, Alonso. Trinculo and Stephano are also represented, as an aging stand-up comic and a homosexual doctor.

Prospero's Books (1991). Dir. Peter Greenaway.

A fanciful and visually lush interpretation of the play, which gives virtually all of the play's lines to Prospero, who is in the process of writing the play as its action unfolds.

Tempest (1992). Dir. Stanislav Sokolov.

A thirty-minute animated version of the play. Part of the HBO series, "Shakespeare's Animated Tales."

The Tempest (1998). Dir. Jack Bender.

This made for television version stars Peter Fonda and John Glover. It transports the play to America during the Civil War.

CLIFFSCOMPLETE READING GROUP DISCUSSION GUIDE

Use the following questions and topics to enhance your reading group discussions. The discussion can help get you thinking — and hopefully talking — about Shakespeare in a whole new way!

DISCUSSION QUESTIONS

1. Some readers and critics have suggested that a more appropriate title for *The Tempest* might be *The Island*. In what ways is a great storm the focus of *The Tempest*? Why might Shakespeare have chosen *The Tempest* as the title? Would the play gain new meaning if it were titled *The Island*?

2. Throughout the nineteenth and twentieth centuries, stage directors have desperately tried to create a realistic storm for the first scene of the play. Real wind and rain, as well as extensive thunder and lightning special effects, have been used with mixed success. More recent productions have tried to make the storm more *symbolic* and *stylized*, relying less on special effects and more on actors to create the impression of a great storm. How important is a realistic storm? What are the benefits of having the actors pretend to be on a boat during wind, rain, and lightning? What is the down side of using minimal special effects? How much of the storm is in the character's mind? In Prospero's mind?

3. Although the setting of *The Tempest* is fictional, scholars debate what type of island inspired Shakespeare to write the play. Some suggest Shakespeare's setting was inspired by popular notions of the Mediterranean isles, while others say Shakespeare was writing about islands of the "New World" (such as Bermuda), which were just beginning to be explored by Europeans during Shakespeare's lifetime. How does the type of island Shakespeare was inspired by affect the meaning of the play? Is the play more or less powerful if we believe that the island in *The Tempest* is part of the "New World"?

4. Directors and set designers for productions of *The Tempest* have often gone to great efforts (and great expense) to create elaborate sets, costumes, and special effects for their productions. How do you envision the island? Is the island fantastical or realistic. How does a realistic setting affect the meaning of the play? What does it add to the play? What does it take away?

5. The character of Caliban can be a major stumbling block for modern productions of *The Tempest*. How much of a wild beast or monster should he be? Often, a black actor is cast and chooses to play the role as a hideous creature. How can a hideous creature also speak some of the most beautiful poetry in the play? What might Shakespeare be saying about the relationship of poetry and wildness? Is it necessary to cast a black actor in the role? How is the character different when played by a white actor? How effective is Caliban as a comic character? As a serious racial symbol? Can he be played for both comic and serious purposes?

6. Several recent productions of *The Tempest* have avoided using special effects of any kind and

have instead focused on the actors' ability to capture the magic of the play. How interesting and powerful would *The Tempest* be without theatrical wizardry? What in the play's characters, language, and situations could communicate the magic in the play?

7. The casting and costuming of Ariel has a long and varied tradition. If you were directing a production of *The Tempest*, would you cast a male or female actor in the role? What are the pros and cons of choosing a woman? A man? Is the character of Ariel asexual? How is the meaning of the play changed if Ariel is played by a black actor instead of a white actor? How would you costume Ariel? Would you use different costumes when Ariel assumes different guises, or would you have the actor playing the role simply use his or her body and voice differently?

8. Some recent productions of *The Tempest* have cast the same actress to play the characters of both Ariel and Miranda. (Vocal recordings and special effects take care of moments when these characters appear together onstage.) How does *double-casting* these roles add meaning to the play? What does double-casting take away?

9. *The Tempest* has been frequently performed for the last 350 years, but few great actors have played the role of Prospero. Although John Gielgud and Patrick Stewart are two notable exceptions, many actors have regarded the role as boring. Is this criticism justified? In what ways is Prospero's choice to forgive and stop using magic as fascinating as the dramatic choices made by other great Shakespearean characters like Macbeth, Lear, or Hamlet?

10. In addition to poetic passages and songs that Shakespeare includes in *The Tempest*, which scenes feel like they could have musical underscoring? What type of music could you use for the following:

* The opening storm
* Prospero dispatching Ariel
* Caliban; Trinculo, and Stephano traipsing about the island
* The vanishing banquet scene
* The wedding masque

11. Although a film of *The Tempest* would allow directors and designers greater opportunity (and perhaps larger budgets) to create spectacular visual effects and costumes, the play has only been filmed a few times and without much critical or popular success. Why do you think *The Tempest* remains a story for the stage? What could a film of *The Tempest* offer that a stage production can't? What does a film production lose?

12. Although historians debate whether *The Tempest* was Shakespeare's last play, it was certainly written near the end of his career. In what ways does Shakespeare say farewell to the stage with *The Tempest*? In what ways does *The Tempest* suggest that Shakespeare was satisfied with his life on the stage? Does the play suggest any possible regrets Shakespeare may have had?

Notes

Index

continued

N

T

Notes

Notes

Notes

Notes

Notes

Notes

Notes

Notes

Notes

Notes

Notes

Notes

CliffsNotes™

CLIFFSCOMPLETE
Hamlet
Julius Caesar
King Henry IV, Part I
King Lear
Macbeth
The Merchant of Venice
Othello
Romeo and Juliet
The Tempest
Twelfth Night

Look for Other Series in the CliffsNotes Family

LITERATURE NOTES
Absalom, Absalom!
The Aeneid
Agamemnon
Alice in Wonderland
All the King's Men
All the Pretty Horses
All Quiet on Western Front
All's Well & Merry Wives
American Poets of the
    20th Century
American Tragedy
Animal Farm
Anna Karenina
Anthem
Antony and Cleopatra
Aristotle's Ethics
As I Lay Dying
The Assistant
As You Like It
Atlas Shrugged
Autobiography of Ben Franklin
Autobiography of Malcolm X
The Awakening
Babbit
Bartleby & Benito Cereno
The Bean Trees
The Bear
The Bell Jar
Beloved
Beowulf
Billy Budd & Typee
Black Boy
Black Like Me

Bleak House
Bless Me, Ultima
The Bluest Eye & Sula
Brave New World
Brothers Karamazov
Call of Wild & White Fang
Candide
The Canterbury Tales
Catch-22
Catcher in the Rye
The Chosen
Cliffs Notes on the Bible
The Color Purple
Comedy of Errors…
Connecticut Yankee
The Contender
The Count of Monte Cristo
Crime and Punishment
The Crucible
Cry, the Beloved Country
Cyrano de Bergerac
Daisy Miller & Turn…Screw
David Copperfield
Death of a Salesman
The Deerslayer
Diary of Anne Frank
Divine Comedy-I. Inferno
Divine Comedy-II. Purgatorio
Divine Comedy-III. Paradiso
Doctor Faustus
Dr. Jekyll and Mr. Hyde
Don Juan
Don Quixote
Dracula
Emerson's Essays
Emily Dickinson Poems
Emma
Ethan Frome
Euripides' Electra & Medea
The Faerie Queene
Fahrenheit 451
Far from Madding Crowd
A Farewell to Arms
Farewell to Manzanar
Fathers and Sons
Faulkner's Short Stories
Faust Pt. I & Pt. II
The Federalist
Flowers for Algernon
For Whom the Bell Tolls
The Fountainhead
Frankenstein
The French Lieutenant's Woman
The Giver
Glass Menagerie & Streetcar
Go Down, Moses

The Good Earth
Grapes of Wrath
Great Expectations
The Great Gatsby
Greek Classics
Gulliver's Travels
Hamlet
The Handmaid's Tale
Hard Times
Heart of Darkness & Secret Sharer
Hemingway's Short Stories
Henry IV Part 1
Henry IV Part 2
Henry V
House Made of Dawn
The House of the Seven Gables
Huckleberry Finn
I Know Why the Caged Bird Sings
Ibsen's Plays I
Ibsen's Plays II
The Idiot
Idylls of the King
The Iliad
Incidents in the Life of a Slave Girl
Inherit the Wind
Invisible Man
Ivanhoe
Jane Eyre
Joseph Andrews
The Joy Luck Club
Jude the Obscure
Julius Caesar
The Jungle
Kafka's Short Stories
Keats & Shelley
The Killer Angels
King Lear
The Kitchen God's Wife
The Last of the Mohicans
Le Morte Darthur
Leaves of Grass
Les Miserables
A Lesson Before Dying
Light in August
The Light in the Forest
Lord Jim
Lord of the Flies
Lord of the Rings
Lost Horizon
Lysistrata & Other Comedies
Macbeth
Madame Bovary
Main Street
The Mayor of Casterbridge
Measure for Measure
The Merchant of Venice

Middlemarch
A Midsummer-Night's Dream
The Mill on the Floss
Moby-Dick
Moll Flanders
Mrs. Dalloway
Much Ado About Nothing
My Ántonia
Mythology
Narr. …Frederick Douglass
Native Son
New Testament
Night
1984
Notes from Underground
The Odyssey
Oedipus Trilogy
Of Human Bondage
Of Mice and Men
The Old Man and the Sea
Old Testament
Oliver Twist
The Once and Future King
One Day in the Life of
    Ivan Denisovich
One Flew Over Cuckoo's Nest
100 Years of Solitude
O'Neill's Plays
Othello
Our Town
The Outsiders
The Ox-Bow Incident
Paradise Lost
A Passage to India
The Pearl
The Pickwick Papers
The Picture of Dorian Gray
Pilgrim's Progress
The Plague
Plato's Euthyphro…
Plato's The Republic
Poe's Short Stories
A Portrait of the Artist…
The Portrait of a Lady
The Power and the Glory
Pride and Prejudice
The Prince
The Prince and the Pauper
A Raisin in the Sun
The Red Badge of Courage
The Red Pony
The Return of the Native
Richard II
Richard III
The Rise of Silas Lapham
Robinson Crusoe